Psychology Aft

Ian Parker has been a leading light in the fields of critical and discursive psychology for over 25 years. The *Psychology After Critique* series brings together for the first time his most important papers. Each volume in the series has been prepared by Ian Parker, features a newly written introduction and presents a focused overview of a key topic area.

Psychology After Deconstruction is the second volume in the series and addresses three important questions:

- What is 'deconstruction' and how does it apply to psychology?
- How does deconstruction radicalize social constructionist approaches in psychology?
- What is the future for radical conceptual and empirical research?

The book provides a clear account of deconstruction, and the different varieties of this approach at work inside and outside the discipline of psychology. In the opening chapters Parker describes the challenge to underlying assumptions of 'neutrality' or 'objectivity' within psychology that deconstruction poses, and its implications for three key concepts: humanism, interpretation and reflexivity. Subsequent chapters introduce several lines of debate, and discuss their relation to mainstream axioms such as 'psychopathology', 'diagnosis' and 'psychotherapy', and alternative approaches like qualitative research, humanistic psychology and discourse analysis. The book as a whole shows how, via a process of 'erasure', deconstructive approaches question fundamental assumptions made about language and reality, the self and the social world. By demonstrating the application of deconstruction to different areas of psychology, it also seeks to provide a 'social reconstruction' of psychological research.

Psychology After Deconstruction is essential reading for students and researchers in psychology, sociology, social anthropology and cultural studies, and for discourse analysts of different traditions. It will also introduce key ideas and debates in critical psychology for undergraduates and postgraduate students across the social sciences.

Ian Parker is Professor of Management in the School of Management, University of Leicester, UK, Visiting Professor in the School of Human and Community Development at the University of the Witwatersrand, South Africa and Co-Director of the Discourse Unit, UK (www.discourseunit.com).

Psychology After Critique

Ian Parker has been at the centre of developments in critical and discursive psychology for over 25 years. The *Psychology After Critique* series brings together for the first time his most important and influential papers. Each volume in the series has been prepared by Ian Parker, presents a concise and focused overview of a key topic area, and includes a newly written introduction which traces the continuing impact of the 'crisis', 'deconstruction', 'discourse analysis', 'psychoanalysis' and 'Lacanian research' inside the discipline of psychology.

Volumes in the series:

Psychology After the Crisis
Scientific paradigms and political debate

Psychology After Deconstruction
Erasure and social reconstruction

Psychology After Discourse Analysis
Concepts, methods, critique

Psychology After Psychoanalysis
Psychosocial studies and beyond

Psychology After the Unconscious
From Freud to Lacan

Psychology After Lacan
Connecting the clinic and research

Psychology After Deconstruction

Erasure and social reconstruction

Ian Parker

Routledge
Taylor & Francis Group

LONDON AND NEW YORK

First published 2015
by Routledge
27 Church Road, Hove, East Sussex BN3 2FA

and by Routledge
711 Third Avenue, New York, NY 10017

Routledge is an imprint of the Taylor & Francis Group, an informa business

British Library Cataloguing in Publication Data
A catalogue record for this book is available from the British Library

Library of Congress Cataloging in Publication Data
Parker, Ian, 1956–
Psychology after deconstruction : erasure and social reconstruction /
Ian Parker.—1st Edition.
pages cm—(Psychology after critique)
Includes bibliographical references and index.
1. Social psychology—Research. I. Title.
HM1019.P37 2014
302—dc23
2014003004

ISBN: 978–1–8487–208–8 (hbk)
ISBN: 978–1–8487–209–5 (pbk)
ISBN: 978–1–3157–708–4 (ebk)

Typeset in Times New Roman
by Swales & Willis Ltd, Exeter, Devon

Printed and bound in the United States of America by Publishers Graphics,
LLC on sustainably sourced paper.

Contents

Series foreword

In the essays collected in these six volumes Ian Parker has brought together for the first time the two radical movements that began in social psychology in the 1960s and 1970s. One of these movements was based on a critical appraisal of the defective methodology of the research programmes that emanated from mainstream American social psychologists. This was rejected for a variety of reasons by a wide variety of critics who shared the belief that people actually deal with what they take to be the meanings of what is happening around them and the significance of the arenas in which actions were performed, according to the rules and conventions of their local social order. The results of a shallow, positivistic approach to discerning the wellsprings of human social behaviour were rejected as sources of reliable knowledge. How people thought, acted, felt and perceived their worlds had little to do with how people actually lived their lives together. People in the stripped-down meaningless worlds of the social psychological experiment were not reacting to stimuli, just trying to make sense of anomic situations with whatever resources their education and history had provided them. People are not empty sites for causal processes but active agents engaged in the tasks and projects that their lives throw up.

At the same time, and for the most part independently, a different kind of criticism was emerging – a display of the moral aspects of the very kind of psychology that was rejected as unscientific by the methodological sceptics. If people believed that psychologists were unearthing the truth about how people thought and acted, then insofar as actual people were unlike this paradigm they would or should strive to achieve it. The realization that such psychology-driven workbooks of human vagaries such as the DSM series of manuals, by presenting a range of ways for human beings to live and act as disorders, defined a kind of person to be emulated who was very much like the bland artefact generated by the statistical methods of the American mainstream, all dissent and difference being ironed out in the deference to some arbitrary level of statistical significance. Critical psychology began to reveal the ways in which the power structures of society and the relations between people from different social classes were brought about. Critical psychology drew from social constructionism the principle that when you can see how something is manufactured you can change it.

The strangest of all the eccentricities of the 'main stream' was the neglect of language. It could hardly be more obvious that the main medium of social interactions is linguistic. Once that is acknowledged the way is open for another dimension – the study of the differences between the linguistically differentiated cultures of the various tribes of humankind. This was not 'cross-cultural psychology' which was merely the transfer of Western middle-class conceptions of life to shape research into the lives of people of very different ways of thinking and acting.

In this elegant introduction to the field of critical psychology Ian Parker shows how gradually but inexorably the two streams began to merge, a process that is continuing. The most striking way in which a critical psychology is currently evolving is in the development of psychology as a moral science. Tied to this insight are explicit studies of the way rights and duties come between natural and acquired tendencies to act and the possibilities that different local moral orders allow: the rapidly growing field of positioning theory.

But all was not plain sailing. The turn to deconstruction, via a reshaping of the linguistic turn to encompass the richer domain of discourse, led to the neglect of the key claim that the 'new psychology' gave socially relative and epoch-specific reliable knowledge, at least pro tem. To reclaim psychiatry from the neurochemists, the place of the active person within a local framework was an essential core to be defended. If persons fade away into clusters of locally contingent selves the key point of the reality of human agency was in danger of being lost.

The second deep insight – perhaps more important than the defence of persons, was relocation of 'mind' to the social network of meaningful interactions, the mind in society. When we learn to abstract ourselves one by one from the social nexus from which each of us emerges we bear with us the indelible mark of our cultural origins. The recoverable content of psycho-dynamics relocates the unconscious to 'what lies between'. In the end we turn back to language and relate symbolic systems not as abstract calculi obeying inbuilt species-specific rules but as the common instruments with which we manage our lives. Psychology can be nothing but the study of cultural-historical-instrumental practices of our ever-changing tribal societies.

The *Psychology After Critique* series is the comprehensive resource we have been waiting for to enable new generations not only of budding psychologists but all those who concern themselves with how we might live, to find their way through the mistakes of the positivistic illusion of a science to a just appreciation of what it might be to come to understand the myriad ways a human being can be a person among persons.

Rom Harré
Linacre College, University of Oxford, UK
Psychology Department, Georgetown University, USA

Series preface

What is psychology? Once upon a time psychologists imagined that they knew the answer to this question. Their object of study, they argued, should be the way that individuals perceive the world, think about it and act in it together with other people. Perception and thinking, in developmental and cognitive psychology, for example, was studied as if it only happened inside the heads of the experimental 'subjects' in scientific laboratories and then 'social psychology' often amounted to little more than an accumulation of the behaviour of those same atomized individuals. The idea that people talked to each other, and that this talk might actually have an effect on the way that people behaved and understood themselves was outside the frame of that kind of academic work.

This series of books is about the consequences of talk being taken seriously, the consequences for scientific investigation and for the way that many researchers today are building innovative new research projects. The discipline of psychology has been transformed since a 'paradigm crisis' erupted nearly half a century ago when pioneers in research into the role of language in thinking and behaviour picked up the thread of early 'radical psychology' critiques which homed in on the limitations of their discipline. The 'paradigm crisis' threw into question the silent world presupposed by the psychologists and launched us all into a world of intense debate over the role of language, of discourse and then of what is shut out of discourse, of the unconscious and of psychoanalysis.

These books were produced in the context of fierce arguments about methods in psychology and over the kinds of concepts we needed to develop in order to do better more radical research. The Discourse Unit was founded in Manchester as a Centre for Qualitative and Theoretical Research on the Reproduction and Transformation of Language, Subjectivity and Practice in 1990. Today it operates as an international trans-institutional collaborative centre which supports a variety of qualitative and theoretical research projects contributing to the development of radical theory and practice. The term 'discourse' is used primarily in critical hermeneutic and structuralist senses to include inquiries influenced by feminism and psychoanalysis. The centre functions as a resource base for qualitative and feminist work, as a support unit for the (re)production of radical academic theory, and as a networking centre for the development of critical perspectives in action research.

We took as our starting point the 'crisis' and the need for critical reflection on the discipline of psychology, the place of psychology and appeals to psychology in other academic disciplines. We then saw the need for a 'critical psychology' that was concerned not only with what went on inside the academic world but also with the way that psychological ideas functioned in the real world outside the universities. The books in this series are written mostly by one individual participant in those debates, but they bring together a number of different arguments for perspectives on the nature of scientific paradigms, deconstruction from literary theory, discourse analysis, psychosocial studies, psychoanalysis and clinical work that were elaborated by researchers in the Discourse Unit.

The books together trace a narrative from the early recognition that language is crucial to understand what is happening in traditional laboratory-experimental psychology – why that kind of psychology is quite useless in telling us about human action – to the development of discourse analysis and the connections with some more radical attempts to 'deconstruct' language from other neighbouring disciplines. A concern with different kinds of psychoanalytic theory – the innovative work now taking place in psychosocial studies – is then introduced to conceptualize the nature of subjectivity. But from the beginning there are some 'red threads' that lead us from the study of language and subjectivity to the study of power and ideology.

These books about psychology as an academic discipline and the increasing role of psychology in our everyday lives are also about the politics of research. And so, when we began to discuss the role of 'deconstruction' or 'psychoanalysis' in the Discourse Unit we always asked whether those other conceptual frameworks would help or hinder us in understanding the connections between knowledge and social change. The books do not pretend to be neutral disinterested description of trends of research in psychology. Our 'crisis' was always about the possibility that the turn to language would also be a turn to more politically engaged – Marxist and feminist – radical reflection on what the theories and methods conceal and what we could open up. The books are accounts of the emergence of key debates after 'the crisis' and sites of 'critical psychological' reflection on the nature of psychology itself.

Ian Parker
Professor of Management in the School of Management,
University of Leicester, and Co-Director of the Discourse Unit
(www.discourseunit.com)

Acknowledgements

This book brings together versions of papers that have either been published in scattered places and are often inaccessible or that are unpublished: Chapter 1 was drawn from my 1999 chapter 'Qualitative Data and the Subjectivity of "Objective" Facts', in D. Dorling and L. Simpson (eds) *Statistics in Society: The Arithmetic of Politics* (pp. 83–88), published by Arnold, reproduced here with permission; Chapter 2 was drawn from my 1999 chapter 'Critical Reflexive Humanism and Critical Constructionist Psychology', in D.J. Nightingale and J. Cromby (eds) *Social Constructionist Psychology: A Critical Analysis of Theory and Practice* (pp. 23–36), published by Open University Press, reproduced here with permission; Chapter 3 was drawn from my 1988 paper 'Deconstructing Accounts', in C. Antaki (ed.) *Analysing Everyday Explanation: A Casebook of Methods* (pp. 184–198), published by Sage, reproduced here with permission; Chapter 4 was drawn from my 2008 chapter 'Constructions, Reconstructions and Deconstructions of Mental Health', in A. Morgan (ed.) *Being Human: Reflections on Mental Distress in Society* (pp. 40–53), published by PCCS Books, reproduced here with permission; Chapter 5 was drawn from my 1999 introduction 'Deconstruction and Psychotherapy' to Parker, I. (ed.) *Deconstructing Psychotherapy* (pp. 1–18), published by Sage, reproduced here with permission; Chapter 6 was drawn from my 1999 chapter 'Deconstructing Diagnosis: Psychopathological Practice', in C. Feltham (ed.) *Controversies in Psychotherapy and Counselling* (pp. 104–112), published by Sage, reproduced here with permission; Chapter 7 was drawn from my 2002 paper which was co-authored (as second author) with Derek Hook (who was kind enough to let me include it now in this book) and published in *South African Journal of Psychology*, 32(2), 49–54, published by Sage, reproduced with permission; Chapter 8 was drawn from my 2003 paper 'Lacanian Social Theory and Clinical Practice', published in *Psychoanalysis and Contemporary Thought*, 26(2), 51–77 by International Universities Press, reproduced here with permission. I have modified some formulations in the published papers and excluded extraneous material. I am, as ever, grateful to Erica Burman and my colleagues in the international network around the Discourse Unit for their critical comments and support during the preparation of this volume. The mistakes must surely in some way be theirs too.

Introduction
Psychology after deconstruction

This book, Volume 2 of the series *Psychology After Critique*, is about a radical twist to social constructionist arguments in the wake of the 'crisis' in the discipline that led us to deconstruct underlying assumptions researchers, including ourselves, were making about the world and about the subjects who make it. 'Deconstruction' became a motif for the unravelling of society and subjectivity applied to developmental psychology, social psychology, psychopathology, psychotherapy and even feminist psychology (Burman, 1998). Dismantling of the internal structure of psychology was quickly connected with deconstructionist approaches in the field of mental health and this gave renewed energy to the task of forging a critical psychology that had something to offer in place of the old mechanistic laboratory-experimental paradigm and the rather sentimental humanistic alternatives emerging inside the discipline (Parker, 2011a). Those connections between debates inside and outside the discipline, between conceptual critique of psychological methods and practical action to tackle distress, showed that many of the objections to deconstruction – that it was only academic, concerned with language, negative – were unfounded. Deconstruction took forward some of the most progressive elements of the crisis debates as we turned from language to discourse to action.

When we founded the Discourse Unit in 1990 deconstruction was already around as one of the resources we wanted to use to enable trans-disciplinary dialogue across the human sciences and debate with those who were subject to psychology as part of the 'psy-complex', the dense network of theories and practices in colleges and clinics through which people are advised, categorized and treated by professionals. While 'discourse analysis' was an opportunity to turn the gaze of critical researchers around from those seen as 'non-psychologists' outside the discipline onto psychology itself – an opportunity to treat psychology as a set of 'discourses' about behaviour and experience – deconstruction helped us focus on the structures of language as structures of power. We found especially useful the theoretical connections between the work of Jacques Derrida (with whom the term 'deconstruction' is usually associated), historical analyses by Michel Foucault of discipline and confession in structures of power in Western culture, and then Jacques Lacan, a psychoanalyst who used and then questioned 'structuralist' approaches to language to develop an alternative to deterministic biologically wired-in accounts of development.

Other books in the *Psychology After Critique* series – on the crisis, on discourse analysis and on different elements of psychoanalytic theory and practice – address important aspects of these ideas in more detail. In this book the chapters focus on the way deconstruction was put to work in relation to qualitative research, mental health politics and psychotherapy, and in this introduction I will describe what attracted us to deconstruction, how it radicalized social constructionist critiques and where it might be leading us now.

Deconstructing what?

A key slogan of the 'paradigm crisis' arguments in psychology at the beginning of the 1970s was 'for scientific purposes treat people as if they were human beings' (Harré and Secord 1972: 84), which raised a number of questions about how to take research and political critique forward. The 'new paradigm' research gathered accounts from people as part of what we now know as the 'turn to language', and it did borrow from some 'structuralist' ideas that were around at that time in other neighbouring social-scientific disciplines. Very quickly, however, this research was supplanted by a 'turn to discourse' that directed our attention to the different contradictory socially structured accounts that people gave of their actions, and it would be tempting to see this development as reflecting the impact of so-called 'post-structuralist' arguments outside psychology (Sarup, 1993).

One of the consequences of that shift from 'language' to 'discourse' in radical research in psychology in the 1980s was that the scientific ambitions of the new paradigm researchers – the argument that we should 'for scientific purposes' treat people as if they were human beings – were lost sight of. Instead, discourse analytic arguments were more closely affiliated with work in the 'sociology of scientific knowledge', and researchers became more interested in studying how scientists talked about what they did – their 'discourse' – than with the aims of science itself (Potter and Wetherell, 1987). Instead of trying to make our work scientific, a distance was struck from science or any other system of knowledge (and, as a correlate of that distance from scientific explanation, a distance from forms of political explanation which were seen as just further 'social constructions').

Another consequence of the shift concerned the place of the human 'subject' in relation to language. The 'new paradigm' valued human agency (Reason and Rowan, 1981), and discourse analysts struggled to maintain a focus on the struggle that individuals have to make meaning while at the same time describing the patterns of meaning that we find in our analyses of discourse. When deconstruction attempted to put dominant terms in language 'under erasure', it seemed to also put the human subject itself under erasure, and it seemed as if post-structuralist theory entailed a form of 'anti-humanism' that was dismissive of agency (Novack, 1983). So, as well as the question of the 'scientific purposes' we follow, there was a question of what the consequences of deconstruction were for what we thought 'human beings' were. In this way, key conceptual issues that were being tackled outside psychology became directly relevant to those of us wanting to develop alternatives inside the discipline.

These debates set the ground for how we understood what 'deconstruction' was for us in our theory and research in psychology. Every journey into deconstruction is different, and a deconstructive ethos is resistant to any attempt to pin 'it' down as if it were a 'method' or a fixed theory of language. Deconstruction was first used in social psychology as a codeword for critique, a way of turning around the attempts to 'reconstruct' the sub-discipline of social psychology and to ask deeper questions about the assumptions researchers still seemed to be making about the nature of theory and research (Parker and Shotter, 1990). A first meaning of 'deconstruction' for us, then, was that it was a process of critique which needed to resist the temptation to rest on secure foundations and build a 'new social psychology' as an alternative to the old. In this way, deconstruction was the equivalent to insisting that the 'crisis' was not resolvable and that we should not pretend to resolve it, to end it. There were good reasons the discipline was in crisis, and we needed to keep that crisis going if we were to keep open spaces for alternatives to emerge, something that is as true today as it was then (Parker, 1989).

Deconstruction focused on binary oppositions that structure the way we think about ourselves and the 'reality' we construct to be able to communicate and relate to each other. The leverage for critique in a deconstruction of these oppositional constructions comes from the way one term is conventionally privileged over the other. For example, 'speech' is privileged over 'writing', so that it seems that speaking is more authentic, original and spontaneous. Writing is then seen as the second-best way of accessing what people really think and what they really want, and psychologists have spent many hours trying to do in practice what philosophers have speculated about, to find a way of developing ways of getting from the writing to what they assume is the real stuff of the inside of the mind of the individual.

When we 'deconstruct' that binary opposition between speech and writing we show, for example, how speech is structured by language itself as a form of writing, that the words we think we spontaneously use to express our inner thoughts pre-existed us and that we cannot communicate without, in some sense, 'writing' new texts out of available resources. More than this, the deconstruction of the opposition forces us to think about each of the terms in a different way. Writing itself is transformed into a kind of textual operation that is creative and open to interpretation, and so when we do 'discourse analysis' of a piece of writing we have to attend to the multiplicity of meanings that are constructed and reconstructed as we try to make sense of it.

These binary oppositions are relatively enduring structures that inform our projects for political and personal change, and so deconstruction was pretty scary not only for those in power, those who benefit from the way reality is structured, but also for those who feel the need for an alternative theoretical structure and tradition from which they can launch their critiques. These oppositions are also fundamental to the whole project of psychology, which is why deconstruction caught on among so many radical researchers in the wake of the crisis.

We began to appreciate another aspect of deconstruction when we treated psychological discourse as one kind of story about individuals and the world that has gained such privilege today, and which is accumulating more status as it becomes globalized and used to interpret the actions and experiences of people outside the specific cultural-political circumstances in which the discipline was developed (De Vos, 2012). A 'deconstruction' of concepts needed to be expanded to take account of the 'lines of force' which held those concepts in place in particular political-economic systems (Derrida, 1981, 1994). The notion of 'development', for example, which has become so central to psychology, defines a trajectory of progress and improvement that does not merely describe how people learn more as they grow but defines a moral good – intellectual and personal 'development' – which we assume each and every individual and culture aims for. The task of conceptual critique is then to ask what is presupposed as the opposite of this 'development' that is privileged, and to explore the value of alternative modes of being that are necessarily, if implicitly and insidiously derogated (Burman, 2008).

Social construction radicalized

An attention to the 'lines of force' that held concepts in place led us to examine the power that psychological explanation has in culture and to a form of 'critical psychology' that aims to challenge that power. There has been much research in the wake of the crisis in psychology that was inspired by the new paradigm qualitative researchers and also by discourse analysts, who showed how this or that aspect of psychology is not discovered as if it were already there but actually 'socially constructed' (Burr, 2003). We cannot take psychological phenomena for granted, assuming that the stories told by psychologists are describing what we really are under the surface of the variety of different accounts we give about ourselves. Instead, we put that psychological explanation and the dominant concepts that hold it in place 'under erasure', and we are thus able to appreciate that we are in fact those varieties of accounts, not something else hidden that only the psychologists can see.

Social constructionist descriptions of the accounts we give of ourselves and of the accounts that the psychologists produce about us have been very useful, and deconstruction radicalizes these social constructionist approaches in psychology by looking at who benefits and who loses when those accounts are deployed, when they are deployed by a professional psychologist as 'models' of psychopathology, for example, or when they are deployed by users of psychological services who are trying to make sense of their own distress (Parker *et al.*, 1995). Deconstruction puts the dominant concepts 'under erasure' when it explores in what ways the supposedly subsidiary or supplemental concept is actually a prerequisite for that dominant concept to function. Psychological knowledge itself, for example, is put under erasure when we explore people's ordinary knowledge about their own psychology, the 'everyday explanation' that they use to make sense of what they do and the reasons why they do it. We can then see how the discipline of psychology is dependent on everyday psychology, draws upon it to develop its theories and models, and cannot function without it.

And, as a consequence of that reversal of priorities so that we value the subordinate term in the process of deconstruction that I have already drawn attention to, we also necessarily question the way we can reinterpret, rework that subordinate term. We do not simply celebrate it, to romanticize everyday explanation as if it were a better kind of psychology, for example, but we examine how it also carries with it sets of assumptions and hierarchies of meaning. Everyday psychology is today, to take a case in point, a form of knowledge which sustains 'psychologization', and some everyday folk are very insistent that they are self-governing individuals independent of social relationships, insisting this against the best efforts of some critical psychologists to persuade them otherwise.

In debates about deconstruction in the realm of mental health and psychotherapy there is then a question of how the practitioner works with everyday understandings organized by a psychologizing discourse which blames the individual for the problem they think they carry within them, respecting those understandings and helping the client to themselves deconstruct it (Parker, 1999b). This is where Foucault's (1975/1979, 1976/1981) work on surveillance and self-monitoring, on the connection between disciplinary power and the idea that we must speak about our secrets to experts, becomes so useful as part of the process of deconstruction. We learnt this from our work with those who suffer psychology, and in the process we learnt that what we came to refer to as 'discursive practice' is so much more than language conventionally understood. And we learnt from debates in psychotherapy that distress is embodied in the experience and actions, physical being and social relationships of those who use psychological knowledge and who find ways to move from social construction to social reconstruction of their own lives.

What next?

Radical conceptual and empirical research has made good use of deconstruction, and it is always asking itself where to go next instead of resting and taking things for granted, including the 'radical' things we think we have learnt. The turn to 'deconstruction' as a radical variant of the social constructionist and discursive movements in psychology was often seen as entailing an attention to the cluster of theoretical approaches that fell under the rubric 'post-structuralism', Foucault's work among them, and so when we are discussing deconstruction itself and the way it goes about tackling oppositional structures of language, we should understand something about the theoretical legacies it carried with it.

The crisis debates had already begun to 'deconstruct' psychology, and they invited into the discipline, or at least into the radical fringes of the discipline and the research centres where change was really happening, a host of new resources. Those resources have in the meantime multiplied, and I address some of them in the course of this book. It is worth mentioning, for example, the contribution of new authors who are reshaping the way we think about psychological research. Let us briefly look at just three of these.

Judith Butler (1990, 1993) has developed an account of 'performativity' which is a little different from the early new paradigm claims that each individual was 'performing' their identity and opinions for specific audiences. The notion of 'performativity' draws attention to the way a reiteration of social categories may or may not be the intentional activity of the individual, but it for sure encourages us to notice the power those social categories have for those involved. Categories of gender and sexual identity, for example, are deconstructed in Butler's work to arrive at the closest we could imagine to a 'queer' psychology. Queer theory after Butler looks for what can be made of the conditions in which we are invited to assume particular identities and it subverts the hierarchies which hold heteropatriarchal structures of power in place.

Ernesto Laclau (1990), together with his co-worker Chantal Mouffe, has developed an account of 'signifiers' – items of meaning in language – and the way they are chained together in discourse to produce versions of reality that have profound political consequences. This is a political theory which was an influential force during the uptake of post-structuralist ideas in British left and feminist culture, and it enabled many activists to 'deconstruct' the assumed status of revolutionary groups that had reproduced a certain model of change at the very same time as they claimed to be breaking from capitalism (Laclau and Mouffe, 1985). This deconstruction drew attention to the way hierarchies of concepts – between the economic 'base' of society which was to be discovered scientifically and the cultural ideological 'superstructure' which deluded people and misled them as to their real interests – were part of hierarchies of power. And, something we can see very clearly now if we think about the attempts to explain what 'false consciousness' of reality is in many orthodox Marxist accounts of ideology, this deconstruction has consequences for how we think about individual psychology (Parker, 2007). The old form of politics Laclau challenged entailed a particular notion of what psychology is – mistaken ideas that only the professionals know how to clear up – and the new form of politics he opened up was concerned with the agency of political subjects as they deconstruct power for themselves.

And Slavoj Žižek (1999) weaves together in an erratic and unpredictable way three specific theoretical resources that have also been important to Butler and Laclau. In the process, Žižek not only deconstructs conventional ideological structures of meaning, but he also pits himself against those others, his dear colleagues who seem to be doing similar work to his. (You might recognize something here of the way those involved in deconstruction after the crisis in psychology are just as critical of each other as they are of the mainstream researchers.) Žižek brings in psychoanalytic ideas from Lacan that were seen as part of the 'post-structuralist' movement, and uses these to question any fixed notion of identity (Parker, 2011b). Žižek draws on Marxist ideas to question what he sees as Butler and Laclau's reformist agenda, the idea that if 'performative' aspects of identity are changed, or 'signifiers' juggled together in a different way, that will be enough. And Žižek links his reading of Marxism and Lacan with an emphasis on the 'negative' moment in Hegelian philosophy (Hegel, 1969). Instead of searching for the way dialectical change proceeds towards a 'synthesis' which resolves the contradictions in reality, his dialectics is always open and subject to new contradictions which will never be resolved. Something rather akin to deconstruction, it seems.

After a journey through deconstruction in psychology and psychotherapy, the final chapter of this book is devoted to a series of debates between these three characters who are not in search of a psychology, and who, instead, remind us that deconstruction aims at the erasure of psychology as conventionally understood so that a social reconstruction of a world that does not need psychology might be possible.

1   Qualitative data and the subjectivity of 'objective' facts

I had 'deconstruction' in mind when writing this little chapter for a book on statistics, though that was not the place to go into Derrida's work, and I made no big deal about it. The role of statistics in psychology is central to the way that researchers in the discipline understand their work as scientists. The reduction of human experience to numbers is taken a step further in statistical representation, and psychology students know well what the mystifying effects of this are when they are subjected to classes which train them to put their 'data' through machinery they cannot understand.

In fact, many psychologists who do quantitative research seek advice from an expert in statistics at some point because they themselves do not really understand what happens in the numerical processing of what they like to think of as their 'findings'. One of the tasks for those of us interested in the social construction of psychological phenomena should be to emphasize the importance of all the debates about interpretation and reflexivity in qualitative research to quantitative research. Tackling the claim of statistics to be 'neutral' or 'objective' is a first step.

So here I deconstruct the dominant opposition between objectivity and subjectivity which makes it seem as if subjectivity is a misleading supplement to real scientific research, and I argue that subjectivity is actually a precondition for any kind of objective standpoint. An 'objective' researcher is actually choosing to adopt a particular kind of subjective position, and so if we do not take that subjectivity seriously as our starting point we will never be able to grasp how objectivity is constructed. This reversal of the privilege given to objectivity thus dismantles the opposition, and enables us to rethink subjectivity as a social construction.

Traditional research directs its attention outward, onto individuals who are not seen as doing research. They are often assumed to be different from us academic 'real researchers'. When we call them our 'subjects' in research studies we are often only using a code-word to cover up the fact that we treat them as if they were objects rather than human beings. Quantitative methods which rely on organizing data statistically lead us to this way of looking at individuals and their problems. This is not to say that quantitative methods necessarily make researchers dehumanize people, but there is a powerful tendency for the systematic fracturing and measurement of human experience to work in this way. That approach also fits with the surveillance and calibration of individuals in society outside the laboratory. Of course, there are researchers who use statistical approaches to combat this, and they try to empower their 'subjects', but they then, of course, have to turn around and look at what the research itself is doing.

This is where qualitative research perspectives are helpful, for they can help us tackle what quantitative researchers say about objectivity and their attempt to see statistics as simply dealing with 'objective facts'. If we do that, then we will see that what research usually takes to be a problem – subjectivity – can actually be turned into part of the research process itself. This would have to be a research practice that studied and conceptualized how the inevitable messiness of social life worked itself through in our action and experience in the world, rather than attempting the rather hopeless task of trying to screen it all out to get a crystal-clear 'objective' picture of the 'facts' that are really there underneath.

Interpretation in qualitative research

Qualitative research is an essentially interpretative endeavour. This is why researchers working in this tradition are often uneasy about including numeric data in their studies or in using computer software to analyse material. This queasiness about numbers is understandable, but there is no reason why qualitative research cannot work with figures, with records of observations, or with statistics as long as it is able to keep in mind that such data does not speak directly to us about facts 'out there' that are separate from us. Every bit of 'data' in research is itself a representation of the world suffused with interpretative work, and when we read the data we produce another layer of interpretations, another web of preconceptions and theoretical assumptions. Numeric data can help us to structure a mass of otherwise incomprehensible and overwhelming material, and statistical techniques can be very useful here, but our interpretations are also part of the picture, and so these interpretations need to be attended to.

Most social research is still deeply affected by empiricism, in which it is believed that the only knowledge worth having in science is that obtained by observation through the five senses (and only the five). The use of laboratory-experimental models to study social issues by predicting and controlling behaviour and measuring it against the behaviour of people in 'control groups', for example, is empiricist (Harré, 1981). A guiding fantasy of the researcher is that they are making 'neutral' observations. The conceptual apparatus of hypothesis testing and falsification in research developed by Karl Popper (1959, 1963) is often wielded by social researchers in defence of 'objective research' of this kind against any use of theory, and especially against theories they most dislike (such as psychoanalysis or Marxism). This is ironic because Popper actually argued for the importance of theory, not as a fixed and final form of complete knowledge but as necessary to enable us to structure our observations so that we might develop a better and better picture as to what the world might be like.

What most quantitative research tries to forget when it pushes aside Popper's arguments about the role of theory is that there is always an *interpretative gap* between objects in the world and our representations of them; there is always a difference between things and the way we describe them (Woolgar, 1988). How we conceptualize that gap is a difficult issue, and there are a range of different positions in traditional philosophy and recent discourse theory to account for the way meaning is produced and structured, and how and where it is anchored (Bhaskar, 1989). This is not the place to go into that further. The point is that research conventionally deals with the problem by wishing the gap way. This 'interpretative gap' returns to haunt research though, and so we need to take it seriously rather than pretend it is not a problem. Definitions of qualitative research which have attempted to respect interpretation rather than wish it away have been cautious about providing a final finished account of what this alternative kind of research is. In one case in psychology, then, three different overlapping definitions are offered, in which it is

(i) An attempt to capture the sense that lies within, and which structures what we say about what we do; (ii) An exploration, elaboration and systematization of the significance of an identified phenomenon; (iii) The illuminative re-presentation of the meaning of a delimited issue or problem.

(Banister et al., 1994: 3)

When we interpret and reinterpret a social issue, we are always bringing ourselves into the picture, and so this is where reflexivity becomes a crucial aspect of the research.

Reflexivity

An attention to reflexivity is sometimes the most difficult aspect of research to tackle because it seems to strike at the heart of the researcher's scientific self-image. That scientific image is often supported by appealing to a 'positivist' account of what real science is (Harré, 1981). Positivism is the dominant approach in much research, and this insists that what we must do is 'discover' things about the world, and treat these things as 'facts' that are independent of us. We are told that empirical observations will identify them and statistical techniques will arrange them in the right order. Positivists often seem to believe that one day we will have set all the facts in their place. This view of science is challenged by philosophers of science and many scientists themselves (Harré and Secord, 1972), but the positivist search for little hard bits of the 'real' still goes on in much mainstream research. Statisticians can too easily be recruited to this endeavour if they do not reflect on what they are doing.

Once again, Popper is recruited to this positivist image of research to defend it against what is often scornfully called 'speculation'. This too is ironic because Popper was himself hostile to positivism, and argued instead that although theoretical frameworks could approximate to the real, they could never finally arrive there. He challenged the idea of total knowledge as arising either from steady fact-gathering or from an all-encompassing theory. There is something very valuable in his account of theory-generation and rational discussion. Good statistical research is a part of that process, and this should be at the heart of how we understand ourselves and how we develop a reflexive critical consciousness of our place in the world. This brings us to a concern with subjectivity and social change.

Subjectivity

Researchers coming across qualitative methods for the first time usually respond to the argument that subjectivity is important in research by saying that they would like to be 'subjective' in their research but that they still have, at the end of the day, to produce an 'objective' report. We need to take care though, for this kind of response falls straight into the trap set by positivist research. The discourse of positivist research positions the researcher such that they experience the issue as if it must entail an opposition between being 'objective' and being 'subjective'. Instead, we should insist that the contrast that concerns us is between 'objectivity' and 'subjectivity'. There is something specific about the nature of subjectivity which differentiates it from the 'merely subjective'. And to put subjectivity at the heart of research may actually, paradoxically, brings us closer to objectivity than most traditional research that prizes itself on being objective.

It is worth stopping for a moment to reflect on the way in which the discourse of positivist research stretches subjectivity and objectivity apart and polices the opposition to devalue interpretation and reflexivity (Parker, 1994). Let us look at two ways the opposition is policed.

Zero sums and 'neutral' positions

First of all the opposition is treated as if it were a zero-sum game, as if the more you have of one the less you can have of the other. The more objective you want to be, so the story goes, the less intuition should be used, the less strongly you should allow yourself to feel about the material. Likewise, if you are making use of your subjective responses to the material, then it seems as if you must necessarily have lost some of the objective value of the research in the process. We are made to play some peculiar rhetorical tricks along the way here, and we call the objects of our research 'subjects' at the very same time as we operate as if we ourselves were objects with no feelings about what we are doing to others. What this process of splitting in research does is to cover over the way in which *our* position enters into research investigation whenever and wherever we do it. If you think about the effort and anxiety that being 'objective' involves, you will quickly realize that you are always doing a lot of emotional *subjective* work.

The very difficulty that some researchers have in maintaining a distance from their objects of study is testimony to the experiential entanglement that starts the minute a research question is posed. Distance and neutrality are themselves aspects of a particular, and often bizarre, subjective engagement with the material. This problem here is made all the worse when that engagement is denied, when we pretend that we think we must have no feelings about the issue we are researching. There is no escape from this, but it is possible to address it by turning around and reflecting upon the subjective position of the researcher. We could think of the paradox here in this way: that the more we strive towards objectivity the further away we drive ourselves, but when we go in the opposite direction and reflect upon our sense of distance we travel towards a more complete inclusive account. In this way objectivity, or, rather, something more closely approximating to it, is approached *through subjectivity* rather than by going against it. This way of addressing subjectivity might seem a little too much like an individual meditative answer to the problem, as if it were a weird paradox from Zen Buddhism. Let us to turn to the second aspect of discursive policing that research engages in to keep subjectivity out. Then we can show how that attention to subjectivity is not simply a kind of delving into the individual self for some mysterious inner truth.

Embedded objectivity and reflexive positions

Positivist research discourse maps subjectivity and objectivity onto an opposition between the individual and the collective. This is the way the trick works. Subjectivity is assumed to be something which lies in the realm of the individual, while objectivity, in contrast, is seen fundamentally as a property of the social order. So, individuals are supposed to have intuitions and idiosyncratic beliefs about things, and they can try to bring these into order by posing hypotheses and testing them out. Meanwhile, the collective, embodied in and exemplified by scientific institutions, absorbs knowledge into a statistically arranged system of truth. A fine balancing act maintains this mapping on both sides of the split between individual subjectivity and collective objectivity, and if either the individual or the collective departs from its assigned position and fails to show those expected characteristics it is quickly and efficiently pathologized. For example, if an individual is too certain about an opinion and starts to take the standpoint of someone with objective truth, then that is seen as some kind of madness. On the other hand, if a collection of people starts to act as if it were endowed with agency and seems to be expressing a will to act in certain ways, then it too is seen as having gone mad (Reicher, 1982; Billig, 1985). In protest movements, individuals who resist too firmly – where they are operating as if they were objective – and crowds that act with too much will – as if they had a subjectivity – are pathologized. This is, in part, because the opposition between the objective and the subjective is itself starting to break down. But even without this breakdown, we can see signs that the mapping of the objective only onto the social and of the subjective only onto the individual is a mistake.

Conceptions of self, for example, that are so different across different cultures are formed out of *social* resources, and they are constructed in relation to others (Shotter, 1993). Investigations of language-learning, memory and cognition in psychology have long indicated that such apparently individual processes are impossible without a network of people around the subject (Middleton and Edwards, 1990). Many of the characteristics that we attribute to individuals, then, are in fact a function of social relationships, and, in turn, social institutions are often modelled upon images of the self. There is, then, an interplay between the two sides of the equation – the individual and the social, and the subjective and objective – that is difficult to disentangle.

Now, the point is that the attempt to approach an objective standpoint through an employment of subjectivity should not be seen as a journey into the private interior of the individual researcher. Rather, reflection upon the position of the researcher is a thoroughly *social* matter and it involves the recruitment and mobilization of networks of people. There is a progressive demystifying dynamic in this reflection which leads towards an engagement with others as part of the research process, and we always need to formulate our research goals *with* those we are researching. Our research will often involve participation and empowerment of a collection of people who are drawn in to produce a type of knowledge that will be useful because it is *connected* to them. The limits to this involvement of others are set, of course, by the institutions in which we conduct research, and the groups involved may be restricted to other researchers. This is a political problem that we need to signal here, something a researcher should reflect upon in any kind of inquiry, but we will have to leave it at that for the moment for other chapters in this book to take up.

'Objective' facts

What we can do is dispose of some of the obstacles that bedevil traditional researchers, and we can treat their problems as opportunities rather than as threats. The activity of the researcher is treated as a problem, for example, in the literature on 'experimenter effects' (Rosenthal, 1966). The neutrality of the investigator was thrown into question by a series of studies which showed that the hypotheses and presence of the experimenter could be so powerful as to shift the data in the desired direction. Techniques which try to solve this problem by increasing the distance between researcher and researched just make it worse, and they certainly make action research which involves people in studies of their own activity impossible. We need to say that of course the researcher affects participants, and is affected by them too in return. Rather than trying to prevent that happening, though, we need to look at *how* it happens and what clues that gives about the nature of the phenomenon under investigation.

We then need to address, as a matter of course, the moral position of the researcher, something that is usually set apart as a peculiar optional extra in traditional research. An ethics checklist is sometimes added onto the research plan as if it were something to be considered *after* the study had been designed. Now, rather than the researcher permitting themselves the luxury of qualms of conscience in an idle moment, as if ethical issues only arise as minor technical hitches, their subjective involvement is something that is to be treated as part of the material under study as a moral question from the start.

Finally, we are able to take due account of the role of language in the research process. Empiricism, which leads the researcher to focus only on observable behaviour, and positivism, which leads the researcher to collect only small discrete chunks of data to process it statistically, together make an engagement with language in research impossible. Many qualitative researchers would argue that since language is the stuff of human experience – that subjectivity is, in large measure, constituted in language – such empiricist and positivist assumptions lead us away from research reality. They are right, for research reality is, in many important respects, *discursive*, and the subjectivity of the researcher is implicated in the same language games as that of the researched (Parker, 1997a). This is why I have referred to the work that positivist discourse plays in leading us into traps which try to make us suspicious of subjectivity. And bringing 'I' and 'we' and 'you' into the narrative of this chapter is an important part of the story. Qualitative research that takes subjectivity and interpretation seriously, then, also demands a new language, a different discourse and different kinds of subject position. Then facts are no longer 'objective' simply because they are in statistical form. Instead, they become things which we understand as embedded in a social world that we continually reproduce, and so they can be transformed as *we* and *you* reflexively connect the process of social research with the people who are represented within it.

2 Critical reflexive humanism and critical constructionist psychology

This chapter tackles the opposition between objectivity and subjectivity, following on from the argument in the last chapter that our deconstruction of the opposition between the two leads us to a quite different notion of what subjectivity itself is. Rather than being the simplistic commonsensical image of subjectivity – as free individual experience – that psychologists like to caricature and set themselves against in their endeavour to be 'objective', our understanding of subjectivity must be more complex.

As we take the next step in the argument in this chapter we see that a deconstruction of the opposition is not just an insistence that one side of the equation that has been derogated should now be celebrated, but that we need to explore the lines of force that condition the way we are invited to understand the way each of the terms is held in place. Here I explore the image of 'humanism' which many opponents of the old laboratory-experimental paradigm resorted to when they complained about the mechanistic reduction of experience in deceptive procedures and quantitative representation. Humanism was assumed by many to express true 'subjectivity' in a discipline dominated by a false 'objectivity' in scientific research.

I draw on the work of Michel Foucault, a figure sometimes associated with Derrida as one of the 'post-structuralist' critics in the human sciences, and use his critique of humanism as a historically specific form to 'deconstruct' it. While many psychologists are suspicious of humanism because it appears to be unscientific, humanism is powerful outside the discipline as the site of individualistic self-actualizing popular psychology. Humanism thus operates as the reversed mirror image of what it opposes, and so I argue that we need to treat it as a social construction. In this way I take reflexivity seriously but deconstruct humanist subjectivity.

This chapter is about the role of humanism, interpretation and reflexivity in critical psychology. *Humanism* has many connotations (depending on what it is being contrasted with), but always emphasizes the status, importance, powers and achievements of people – rather than emphasizing, say, the sociocultural resources they draw upon. In psychology, humanism is associated with holistic approaches to the person which emphasize the subject's agency, rationality and awareness. Of course, we would like to be subjects of this kind, as close as possible to things in the world and to the things we do, selfpresent and transparent to our own natures. The problem is that as soon as we start to use language, our experience becomes mediated and complicated. The discourses and practices that make it possible for us to be human beings in a culture make any understanding we have of ourselves ambiguous and confused. Things and events do not speak directly to us. Human life is necessarily complex and contradictory and so we need to *interpret* what is going on. Common sense is not adequate to this task, since it is precisely commonly used language that betrays and misleads us when we try to use it to understand ourselves; instead, we must use theory.

One of the key contributions of constructionism in critical psychology is that it draws attention to the way discourse works ideologically. This is why some of us draw upon Michel Foucault's (1975/1979, 1976/1981) description of the emergence of certain 'regimes of truth' which seem to give us clear and simple answers about our nature, but actually bind us all the more firmly into relations of power. If we adopt this kind of critical constructionist approach, humanism is problematic – and humanistic psychology even more so. Humanism appeals to a 'self' under the surface that can be transparent to itself and communicate directly with others (Knight, 1961; Ayer, 1968). Foucault's work suggests that this 'self' serves an ideological purpose, bolstering the illusion of free and equal communication which helps to mask the operation of power. Nevertheless, in this chapter I will argue that we still need to hold to some variety of humanism, one that is grounded in an understanding of social practice, if we want to do progressive work in and against the discipline. This will necessitate taking the role of interpretation seriously, both in our understanding of ourselves and in our analysis of the social construction of our psychology. It also requires us to be *reflexive* when we use theory: to make our theories and analyses able to accommodate our *own* selves and activities.

Along with culturally grounded humanism and theoretically informed interpretation, then, we need a form of critical reflexivity. Foucault is often treated as an archetypal antihumanist (e.g. Racevskis, 1983) and is used quite correctly to argue against the 'rational unitary subject' of mainstream psychology (Henriques *et al.*, 1998). Nevertheless, I will argue that his work is helpful here, for it provides a way of reflecting on discourse which is embodied, sensitive to forms of power and able to connect theory and practice. Towards the end of the chapter I will outline three themes which flow from these arguments and which should be part of a critical reflexive humanist approach in constructionist psychology.

Problems in psychology and in humanist alternatives

Psychology is about problems. That is to say, the motive behind most research in psychology is a struggle to understand something that does not seem quite right, to make sense of an issue that is problematic. Sometimes that struggle to understand involves problematizing, making strange something that appears too self-evident, too coherent. Then we have to break down the phenomenon into its component parts to see what they do and where they come from.

Breaking up is hard to do

This is where critical research comes in. The dynamic of debates over alternative critical approaches in psychology has been to direct our attention inward at psychology itself, and the struggle to understand how the discipline works and where it comes from is a vital part of critical reflexive work (Prilleltensky and Fox, 1997). Yet there is a paradox here, for critical researchers have often been concerned with a holistic understanding of phenomena and a respect for the integrity of experience. Mainstream psychology has been dehumanizing in its theory and practice, and so humanism has become attractive as an alternative. We find humanism advanced as a 'third force' in North American psychology in the 1960s (Wann, 1964; Bugental and Thomas, 1967), and humanist sentiments are important in the 'new paradigm' arguments later on. We find some version of humanism, for example, in the demand that we should 'for scientific purposes treat people as if they were human beings' (Harré and Secord, 1972: 18), and in the attention to subjectivity in qualitative research (e.g. Reason and Rowan, 1981; Banister *et al.*, 1994).

Ethnomethodology, symbolic interactionism and ordinary language philosophy were among the microsociological resources mixed together in the new paradigm (Harré, 1979). Researchers who have had some contact with sociology are often dismayed to find that ideas that seem so innovative to psychologists – and now much qualitative research, discursive psychology and social constructionism is added to the list – are actually quite old, recycled items. A lack of attention to coercion and conflict still marks some recent appropriations from sociology, including ideas from the sociology of scientific knowledge and conversation analysis (Potter and Wetherell, 1987; Edwards and Potter, 1992; Antaki and Widdicombe, 1998). We need to hold onto these issues, to appreciate that when language is structured into discourses it is structured such that spaces are permitted for certain things to be said by certain people, and such that certain subject positions are allowed and others proscribed. Phenomenology has been an important resource in these arguments, for it urges us to focus on the meanings that people make and on the varieties of experience of living as psychological beings (Richardson and Fowers, 1997). This focus, and the respect for individual meaning-making, characterizes both the worst and the best of humanism.

Breaking with humanism

It seems to be in contradiction to humanist values to demand that we should break things up, that we should pull apart our discipline and its methodological apparatus in the name of good critical research. We can address this paradox in two ways, beginning with the understanding that it is not good enough to turn to a simple humanism as a reaction to the mechanistic picture of people which is peddled by traditional psychology. Such simple humanism does not tend to question the way in which subjectivity is constructed because it is so concerned with respecting people's experience. If we want to challenge the dehumanization of 'subjects' by the discipline we cannot take experience, and the meaning people attribute to things, at face value.

The first reason why it would be a mistake to do so is that all too often we find psychological models and processes reproduced in miniature in people's everyday lives. Many critical researchers who take a social constructionist position argue that this is not because those models and processes are real and psychology has 'discovered' them, but rather that psychological knowledge is now part of the structure of common sense (Harré, 1983; Shotter, 1993). When people talk about accessing their memory as if it were a storage machine, or about debugging relationships as if they were systems, for example, they are doing precisely that, talking about their experience and behaviour in a particular way. Cognitive psychology and computer modelling may then seem appropriate to understand those mental processes, but we need to explore where that talk has come from in the first place instead of assuming that we have revealed something about thinking. Similarly, when people talk about family rivalries in their childhood to explain their experience, or refer to unconscious reasons for things they do, we need to ask where those ways of talking come from and what function they serve.

There is a point here that we will pick up again later on, which is that the accounts that people give of their own and others' mental states are structured. The advantage of social constructionism in psychology is precisely that it homes in on that question, rather than taking psychological phenomena on good coin as they appear directly and immediately to us. We need some theoretical understanding of how they are structured, what role they play in culture, and what role psychology plays in forming those accounts. It is most important, too, that we hold onto the point that our research should focus on the accounts themselves rather than discovering hidden mental machinery beneath the surface.

The second reason why we cannot take experience and meaning at face value is that we thereby miss or gloss over the very work of contradiction in psychology. For all the competition between the two, popular humanism shares with psychology the idea that coherence or consistency is the bedrock of human reality and of good theory about it. In humanist defences of human beings against socalled scientific explanations of behaviour this is played out in the figures of 'integrity', 'growth' or 'self-actualization' (e.g. Rogers, 1961; Maslow, 1973). In mechanistic psychological investigations which often violate human understanding we see it played out in the obsession with consistency in theories or assessment schedules. The principle of 'parsimony' in psychological theorizing, in which the simplest, most economical explanation for phenomena is favoured, is just one expression of the attempt to filter out the messiness of mental life and the complex accounts we develop to make sense of it. Contradiction, inconsistency, ambiguity and ambivalence are the stuff of human psychology, and once we can take them on board we can better understand why the discipline of psychology is itself so incoherent and fragmented.

The problem with humanism is exacerbated when it becomes turned into a humanist psychology (e.g. Rowan, 1994; Greening, 1998). Humanist values are crucial to any hope for progressive social change, and they underpin Marxist critiques of dehumanization in capitalist society, for example (Novack, 1983). However, in the hands of psychologists, they become a warrant for the reduction of social processes to the level of the individual (e.g. Nevill, 1977). It is for this reason that feminists, who have helped to maintain humanist values in a dehumanizing world, have been scathing about what humanistic psychology does to devalue connections between women's experience and political struggle (e.g. Lerman, 1992; Waterhouse,

1993). We need to contrast humanistic psychology, which performs the same kind of ideological victim blaming as the rest of the discipline, with the standpoint of a more complex critical humanism.

Reflexivity, politics and power in psychological research

One of the symptoms of relativist discourse in psychology is that there is often a simple appeal to 'reflexivity' to solve problems of politics and power in the discipline (e.g. Potter, 1998). Some writers in the tradition of discourse analysis also appeal to reflexivity even though they are otherwise extremely suspicious of anything that looks therapeutic, to the extent that talk of subjectivity of any sort is accused by them of slipping into humanistic psychology. Reflexivity is often felt to be a kind of space that we can escape into, as if we could then look upon the discipline from a distance, or reflexivity is sometimes even thought to be a solvent, in which the abusive aspects of psychology can be dissolved. The activity of thinking back and thinking around an issue, and situating oneself, which is a valuable and necessary part of deconstructive and discursive therapeutic work, is thought to illuminate all problems and, in that very process, solve them.

I am caricaturing a bit here of course, but what I want to draw attention to is the mistake sometimes made by radicals in the discipline when they imagine that to simply turn around and reflect on what we are doing, as researchers or practitioners, is enough. I should also quickly point out that I am not impugning critical reflection on our practices, and I want to draw a contrast between reflexivity as such and a critical reflection. While reflexivity is something that proceeds from within the interior of the self, and participates in all of the agonizing confessional work that Foucault (1975/1979, 1976/1981) so brilliantly describes, critical reflection traces the subjective investments we make in our everyday practice, and traces them to the networks of institutional power that contain us. While reflexivity can be a passive contemplative enterprise that all too often succeeds in paralysing the individual as they take responsibility for the pain and troubles of a painful and troubling set of circumstances, critical reflection is an active rebellious practice that drives the individual into action as they identify the exercise of power that pins them into place and the fault lines for the production of spaces of resistance.

Foucault, practice and counterpractice

Some of the most critical work in psychology threatens to fall into passive reflection on the discipline, and this even goes on in the name of an analysis of power and resistance. A case in point is the way in which Foucault's work is sometimes reinterpreted, so that instead of being a threat to power it becomes an avoidance of political action (e.g. Minson, 1980; Soyland and Kendall, 1997).

Foucault is particularly important to us because his description of surveillance and confession in Western culture, which accounts for the development of the 'psy-complex' (Ingleby, 1985; Rose, 1985), comes from the very heart of the discipline. It is often forgotten that Foucault was a psychologist by training, and that his analysis of individual identity was grounded in clinical experience in psychiatric wards and prisons (Parker, 1995). Foucault's work marks a turning point both in the way that the objects of psychology may be conceptualized and in the methods we may use to understand those objects. His founding concerns were how we understand and experience abnormality and distress. The ways we account for different modes of psychological function must now also include a reflection upon the network of classifications that divide what is normal from what is not (Parker *et al.*, 1995). Psychology is a powerful actor in this network, a network Foucault saw as made up of what he termed 'dividing practices'. His approach emphasizes the ways in which the theory and practice of psychology meet in correctional, therapeutic and welfare settings to specify how personal experience is to be defined and treated.

The ways we conceptualize the work of psychology, and the significance of what Foucault (1977) was to call 'counterpractice' in and against the discipline, also reminds us that he was an exemplary 'engaged intellectual'. Many of us now using his work in psychology have come to see that it just not possible to do so in good faith unless we also develop a counterpractice. The organization Psychology Politics Resistance is the product of many different strands of political opinion (Reicher and Parker, 1993), but important among those strands is the spirit of Michel Foucault. It is appropriate that this is how his work as academic and activist appears again today in the world of psychology.

I would want to hold onto some variety of reflexive activity as prerequisite for, and necessary accompaniment to politics outside and inside psychology. The critical reflection I have described carries with it the best and most progressive elements of reflexivity. Like any other approach, we use Foucault as part of a transitional strategy to bring psychologists up against the barriers to change in the discipline. Foucauldian discursive approaches assist that activity of reflection on the barriers constructed in the institutional discourse of psychology.

Constructing critical reflexive humanism in psychology

We have arrived at the point where we can draw together some of the problems that psychology poses and reconstruct them as issues that critical research can address. Perhaps one of the main outcomes of this process of critical reflection on the way psychology inhibits the work of interpretation is that it allows us to formulate more clearly what more we want out of good research. When the discipline defines what 'science' is in a restricted way, which pretends to model itself on the natural sciences, it also defines what desires we permit ourselves to express, and, as a consequence, we can easily forget what led many of us into psychology in the first place.

Let us conclude, then, with a review of key points for a critical constructionist psychology. Some versions of discursive psychology that have been imported from psychology's close neighbours, in particular from sociology and micro-sociology, have often failed to take these issues seriously, and sometimes we have just been left with something that masquerades as a progressive alternative but is actually dismissive of the problems psychology poses and itself maintains. I will describe three components to more useful research.

Agency and social action

We need to take subjectivity seriously, but we need to take that a step further to look at how the subjectivity of the researcher affects and interconnects with that of the researched, and, in particular, what forms of agency are facilitated or blocked in the process. An attention to subjectivity should not be a licence for individual navelgazing, and this means that it should be considered as a relational issue, not one that simply resides in the individual. There have been attempts to emphasize agency in alternative psychology over the last decade, but often the appeal to the individual has been too simple and voluntaristic.

While symbolic interactionism has made a useful contribution to psychological notions of selfidentity, and drawn attention to the ways in which meanings are shared symbolic resources (Mead, 1934), we need to be cautious about the conceptions of agency that have been imported with it. It is all too easy to simply assert that human beings are endowed with agency, or even to say that this is produced out of interaction with significant others. A further step should surely be a thorough account of the ways in which different forms of consensus are maintained in symbolic interaction, and the way agency operates as much through resistance as through the uncomplicated exercise of a mysterious human gift. The attention to subjectivity, then, leads us to ask for fairly sophisticated accounts of agency.

Interpretation and theory

If we are to take as our starting point the always already interpreted nature of social and psychological reality, we need to take the next step and look for theoretical frameworks that can assist in comprehending accounts. Interpretation is guided by implicit theories of the self and the world even when one tries to avoid theorizing. For example, one of the mistakes of ethnomethodology (drawn in from microsociology during the paradigm crisis debates) was to pretend that one could dispense with grand theory because it always reified activity and treated 'accomplishments as things' (Garfinkel, 1967). This refusal of theory leads us into mere descriptions of behaviour, which all too often amount to little more than mindless empiricism (Harré, 1981).

Psychologists who turn to critical research sometimes eschew theory altogether, as a reaction to the dehumanizing models of human beings that they have had to put up with. The assertion of a simple humanism and defence of uncomplicated subjectivity against psychological fake science sometimes then goes alongside a refusal to develop any account which does not completely accord with the immediate felt life experience of research participants. Ethnomethodology is one of the end points, one of the cul de sacs, of this line of reasoning. An understanding of the power psychological models enjoy cannot be developed if you refuse to go beyond everyday accounts, and if you treat all theory as totalizing and reifying. So, as a way of managing the interpretative gap we need to develop useful theory.

Reflexivity, knowledge and power

The accounts we gather in critical research, the language we study, and the language we study it in, are all forms of knowledge which distribute rights to know and rights to speak to different people in different social positions. The role of science, for example, as a master discourse, a form of knowledge which is privileged over common sense is very much at issue in psychology as a discipline which likes to think of itself as a science. There have been attempts to conceptualize the relationship between different forms of knowledge, and the ways in which the distribution of representations of the world operates ideologically to open up or close down certain forms of action. The shift from individual cognition to the study of shared 'social representations' in an influential current of French research has been particularly important, to the extent that writers in the 'new paradigm' claimed that they too were always studying social representations. There is also a concern with the ways reified and consensual forms of knowledge function in society, and give to social actors frameworks to understand themselves (Moscovici, 1976/2008).

Nevertheless, it must be said that much of this work tends to reify science as if it were a special knowledge rather than look at the institutions in which it is embedded, the ways in which it operates in the service of power through discursive practices; and we need to take care not to idealize consensual universes as the 'other' to science. All forms of knowledge need to be thrown into question, treated as problematic, and we need to attend to the way knowledge is intertwined with power. This would be a third component of good empowering research.

Social constructionism has been invaluable to the development of critical psychology, and it invites us to reflect on the way each and every psychological experience we have is constituted in forms of discourse and practice rather than given and to be taken for granted. It leads us to interpret the complexity of human life and ask how it has come to be the way it is rather than adopting assumptions that are relayed through common sense and which then feel as if they must be true. It also means that if we are to be humanist in our work we have to be so in a more theoretically sophisticated way than is advocated by humanistic psychology. We need a complex humanism, a good deal of interpretation underpinned by theories which take power seriously, and a critical reflexivity which is embodied and grounded in forms of practice.

3   Deconstructing accounts

This chapter includes an early worked example of deconstruction which was designed to show how the approach can be 'applied' to a piece of text. I was invited to write it for a book on 'everyday explanation' in the mid-1980s, and there are some aspects of the chapter that are useful reminders of a particular historical moment in the paradigm 'crisis' debates in social psychology when the 'turn to language' was itself beginning to turn into a 'turn to discourse'.

You will notice that I refer to 'post-structuralism' as if it really was a complete theoretical package, and this gives me an opening to link the deconstruction of conceptual oppositions to deconstruction of power. The chapter was for a book that was itself an intervention into social psychological understandings of accounts that people give of their own experience, and there was an attempt in the book (which was sympathetic to the 'new paradigm' qualitative researchers) to shift attention from the accounts that psychologists gave of other people's behaviour (those outside the discipline commonly supposed to be 'non-psychologists') to the accounts people themselves gave. Also notice the way I formalize deconstruction here as if it was a procedure that could be followed through particular 'steps'. It seemed at the time that I had no choice but to do this in order to make the approach accessible to psychologists who like 'methods', but it makes me cringe a bit today.

I aimed to show how techniques developed in literary theory could be 'applied' to everyday explanation. However, as you will see when we come to the empirical example, the deconstruction of a piece of text involves a radical overturning of traditional social-scientific distinctions between what are 'ordinary' spontaneous accounts and what is extraordinary, manufactured script, script as psychological writing itself is.

The emergence of a deconstructive approach to social psychology should be understood in the context of attempts to provoke a paradigm shift in the discipline over a decade ago. At the time, critics of traditional laboratory-experimental social psychology hoped to reconstruct the discipline out of the ruins of the crisis-ridden 'old paradigm' (Armistead, 1974; Harré and Secord, 1972).

The 'crisis' in social psychology developed primarily out of a claim that most published research was trivial, presented a mechanistic model of the human being, and failed to engage meaningfully with real issues and experiences. We have to be aware, though, that other (as yet unresolved) problems played a role. Most important was the question of power: power as a pervasive quality of social interaction (highlighted in the classic obedience and conformity experiments), power as a profound influence on laboratory results (demonstrated in the work on experimenter effects and demand characteristics), and power inherent in the situation of a privileged researcher vis-à-vis his (and sometimes her) subjects. The phenomenon of power is a difficult one to conceptualize without appreciating the ideological status of social psychology in our culture. In turn, to understand the work of ideology we have to appreciate the power of language, which is where 'new paradigm' social psychology really made its mark.

New social psychology

Language, the proponents of the new paradigm argued, was the key to understanding social life. Psychology mistakenly viewed itself as a natural science, and, on top of that, it had a mistaken view of how the natural sciences obtained knowledge of their objects. Instead, psychology (and especially social psychology) should recognize that the pre-eminent role of language, of meaning, in social action necessitates a turn to the human sciences, and that a more adequate ('realist') model of inquiry could be adopted. There are, of course, two lines of attack here. The first stresses the difference between natural science and human science and tries to shift psychology from one to the other. The second stresses the value of methods actually employed in the natural sciences and tries to bring psychology up to date. There is a creative tension between the two positions advanced in the new paradigm. At the risk of caricaturing them and glossing over their points of convergence, it is useful to identify hermeneutic and structuralist strands.

The *hermeneutic* strand focuses on the ability of the social actor to produce meaning, to construct new definitions of a situation and to communicate intentions and the import of action to others. Social life is constituted by the accounts which we must give one to the other to maintain the peculiarly human quality of the world. Inquiry into the life world of social actors requires an empathetic involvement in, and elaboration of, the 'hermeneutic circle' of meaning. In this view, then, the formal properties of interaction are no more than interpretations, constructions of an interested observer, and have no other existence (Shotter, 1975, 1983, 1984).

The *structuralist* strand, in contrast, makes a determined effort to uncover the patterns of interaction, the structures which inform the activities of social actors. Accounts are gathered, 'negotiated', with those being studied because the accounts and actions have the same source. Accounts are used, then, to reconstruct a social world of which each individual actor has an imperfect, fragmentary knowledge. In this way, the researcher takes note of the explanations of action given by people and arrives at a deeper understanding, following the methods of 'realist' science, of the formal properties of the chosen social world (Harré, 1979; 1983; Marsh *et al.*, 1974).

The debate between the two sides of the new paradigm echoes longstanding and unresolved conflicts in social psychology between agency and structure (Harré, 1983; Shotter, 1980). What both tendencies in the new paradigm have neglected, however, is the way interpretation, conflict and resistance in social life cry out for an analysis of meaning in terms of *power*. We are able to put these issues to the forefront of our research if we adopt a deconstructive approach to texts, and move beyond the dichotomy between structuralism and hermeneutics. Deconstruction uncovers the way language, and the analysis of the texts we weave with language, works.

Deconstruction

While the arguments over the nature of the paradigm shifts which fuelled the crisis inside social psychology were burning, intense debates were also raging in the other human sciences. These debates, which filtered through into some of the formulations of our own new paradigm critics, revolved around the value of structuralism and post-structuralism as ways of understanding language. In literary theory, where the conflict between the different positions was most intense, the transition from structuralism to post-structuralism also saw the emergence of a deconstructive approach to texts (Eagleton, 1983). There is some value in attending to these debates because we can then use them to extend the work of the new paradigm writers in social psychology, arrive at a more productive understanding of the nature of texts, and gain a better understanding of the relationship between explanations and power. In order to appreciate the value of deconstruction in social psychology, we have first to deconstruct structuralist and hermeneutic approaches.

Language, according to structuralism, should be understood as a system – a system in which each item, or word, gains its meaning only by way of its differences from the other items (Saussure, 1915/1974). Intentions we express are immediately caught up in the web, system and structure of language and escape our grasp. The structuralist approach to language, then, sets up an opposition between the 'system' of the language as a whole (a structure which would be uncovered by an investigator) and the 'use' of that language by individuals (the day-to-day occasions when the words are transmitted). The first is studied and the second studiously ignored by a structuralist.

The value of structuralism, for literary theorists, was that it directed attention to the underlying pattern of a piece of writing. Whereas the old interpretative tradition had attempted to trace the meanings in the text to the intentions of the author, the structuralist approach was able to produce a rigorous explanation of the way the text worked. At an extreme, such an approach was supposed to involve the conceptual 'death of the author' (Barthes, 1977). While the conclusions they drew about the irrelevance of individual intention and agency were not, of course, shared by social psychologists interested in structuralism in the new paradigm, the model of language they adopted was taken up.

However, if you pursue that argument you will eventually arrive at the breakdown of strictly structuralist notions and their collapse into post-structuralism. It is, in short, possible to deconstruct the opposition between the structure of language and its use. Each person constructs an imperfect, fragmentary, idiosyncratic version of the structure which affects the relation between the words each time she or he communicates with another person. In addition, each act of interpretation requires the reproduction of the system of language and, crucially, the production of new metaphors which disrupt the system (Derrida, 1981).

The lesson I as a social psychologist take from these developments is that any text I would want to examine is open to further interpretation. The meanings in a text shift from one moment to the next, and according to its wider context. A reading of the text, then, is provisional and is profoundly affected by my own and your prior understanding and expectations (themselves aspects of experience which are impossible to definitively fix as if there are confounding variables). The most that can be done is to persuade you that my interpretation indentifies what is going on.

The obvious escape route from the relativism into which these debates seem to be dragging us has already, of course, been closed off. We cannot ask the authors what they 'really meant'. But what of the authors of social texts such as speech, conversations and explanations? Here, the development of deconstruction in literary theory is particularly useful. It places into question the status of intention in the production of language.

An obvious, and appealing, way of marking the difference between literary theory and social psychology is to say that there is a crucial distinction to be drawn between writing and speech. Writing is constructed in such a way as to meet the expectations of a number of readers, and it can be interpreted in many ways as time flows on and as it becomes progressively detached from the experience and memory of the author. We believe that speech is different; it expresses thought, and as part of the accountability of conduct it is immediate and more spontaneous. The experience of speaking is one which leads us to imagine that speech flows more directly from what we really want to mean.

Speech, though, is constructed so as to be a communication to others. The language used as the medium of communication both facilitates and moulds what we say. We cannot invent anew terms to express our intentions. On the contrary, we find ourselves using words which have been repeated many times before. Old words in new contexts obtain their meaning from their identity with the way they were last used, and their difference from the way were used before. Neither the language nor the context can be controlled by, or traced to, the intention of an individual. Is not speech, in fact, a variety of writing? This is the conclusion we might arrive at when we deconstruct the opposition between writing and speech. In turn, this warrants our use of the term 'text' to denote both written and spoken forms of language production (Derrida, 1967/1978).

As far as social psychology is concerned, the focus on texts as our objects of inquiry should enable us to produce interpretations which are intrinsically social. Our deconstruction of an item of text is a way of arriving at interpretations which are locked into the surrounding social context. I take this as an opportunity to raise general issues about the way texts re-place us in positions of power. Each specific deconstruction is illustrative of, and gives more leverage to, a deconstruction of social relations.

I must confess that I am loath to formalize the deconstruction of theoretical positions into an abstract method which can be applied to 'non-theoretical' texts. Strictly speaking, deconstruction is not a method in the sense of being a set of techniques (Derrida, 1981). However, it is possible to summarize three steps or stages to a deconstruction (Wood, 1979).

The first step is to identify conceptual oppositions, or polarities, in the text, and the way one pole is privileged over the other. In the case of structuralism the key dichotomy was between structure and use. In the case of hermeneutics I pointed to the opposition between speech and writing. In the course of this chapter, I want to draw attention to further conceptual oppositions: between what is spontaneous and what is scripted; between what is real and what is fictive; and between what is to be counted as everyday and what as theoretical explanation. In the empirical example, I will draw attention to further oppositions which will serve as devices to highlight processes at work in the text: between metanarrative and narrative; between reflection and subjectivity; and between recasting and casting.

The second step is to demonstrate that the privileged pole of the opposition is dependent on, and could not operate without, the other. We bring the hitherto subordinate concept to the fore. In the case of structuralism, then, the use of language profoundly affects the structure, thus making capture of the structure of a language impossible. In the case of hermeneutics, writing is brought forward as a model of speech, making invalid the traditional linking of speech and intention. The consequences of a deconstruction involve, I hope to show as we proceed, a re-emphasis in social psychology on scripted, fictitious and theoretical items of text over what we currently understand as being spontaneous, real or everyday forms of explanation. We will see, when we come to the empirical example, the importance of narrative, subjectivity and casting in the production of a text by social actors.

The third step involves a reinterpretation of the opposition, and the production of new concepts. In the cases of structuralism and hermeneutics, we arrived (implicitly) at the notions of text and deconstruction. The third step, however, requires an intervention into the production of the text (Derrida, 1981). For social psychologists, this calls for the production of new practices (and new problems for those wanting to stick to the text, as we shall see).

A deconstruction of a piece of text carries with it assumptions about the nature of meaning, and it produces new meanings out of the texts it contacts. It changes what it studies. In addition, the way I read a text is informed by the moral/political structure of the interpretation (the scene, which in this case is an academic paper), and the experiences I bring to it (which result from my participation in the production of other academic and non-academic texts). These factors give power to an interpretation, and may boil down to relations of power between those who are permitted to construct 'real theories' and those who are deemed to produce 'everyday explanation'.

Empirical example

For our text we have an item of script in which the social actors contest the nature of the distinction between reality and fiction, and the power of theory over everyday life. We will see one character attempt to construct a metanarrative and implicitly reflect and recast the other within it. We will also address the issue of implicit explanation.

The nature of text

The idea of 'text', which lies at the heart of deconstruction, and which emerges from the wreckage of structuralist and hermeneutic styles of new paradigm social psychology, has a number of useful and exciting qualities.

Any text – be it a speech, a monologue or a treatise – consists of a number of warring themes. The conflicts between the poles of any conceptual oppositions that we might uncover need not necessarily be identified with conflicts between persons. In fact we would expect that were a number of characters to congregate to debate differences, each person would slip from one position to the next, exploiting ambiguities and loopholes in the other's argument. However, the stuff of everyday explanation is in the interchange of opinion. Most of the talk that people engage in is in the presence of others. We will, then, examine a text which is wrought through dialogue. Here, the different positions adopted will be easier to define and explore.

A notion we may draw from the new paradigm is that the utterances of social actors have an overwhelmingly expressive function (Harré, 1979; Shotter, 1984). When social life is viewed as self-presentation through ingeniously constructed rhetorics, or it slips into well-worn rituals, we are right to use the notion of a 'script' to highlight what is happening. Once we have deconstructed the distinction between speech and writing, however, we can go further than this. We then have a licence to turn to scripts themselves. Written scripts need be no less spontaneous than real speech. The text in this example once had the status of a script. The objection might be made that such a text is not 'real'; it is fiction. Some fictions, however, are more real than others. The explanations we give to others – the texts we pass on – are sometimes mistaken, sometimes half-truths, occasionally deliberate lies. Some items of fiction are lived by large numbers of people in a culture, and the meanings are discussed and contested. They have effects as real as ostensibly unscripted non-fictitious explanations. They operate as an ideology.

Furthermore, a problem with much research in social psychology is that it illuminates a social world we do not implicitly know. Readers of such reports can only either take what the research says on trust or retreat into a cynical suspension of all accounts. A deconstruction should be open to revision. An interpretation should be reopened as times and contexts change. Readers should have some space at the margins of even an academic text.

Sample texts

We do know the social worlds of soap operas. Sociologists have turned in recent years to analyse the way audiences receive these worlds and incorporate the narratives into their own worlds. In the case of American television series, the preoccupations and antics of the characters become templates for the understanding of the non-soap world, metaphors for the lives of politicians, and frames to organize explanations. The advantage the soap has over discrete narratives is that actors develop a history and are attributed with personality traits and intentions.

Although the most popular television soaps have the advantage of having a large audience in many countries, their status as texts presents problems for a deconstructive analysis. There are the meanings of clothes, scenes and locations which could be treated by semiological analysis. There are also the non-verbal cues which supplement, organize and occasionally contradict the spoken message. For these reasons I have taken a piece of text from an (English) radio soap.

The Archers, which has been running on BBC Radio 4 since 1950, has developed a minor cult following in the past few years. Radio 4 is the 'serious' channel of the BBC. From being a fairly traditional serial, *The Archers* has roused controversy with the introduction of social issues. Letters to Radio 4 news programmes and *The Guardian* (a liberal middle-class newspaper) discuss the fate of characters and the corruption of the series by the unpleasant practices and vices which feed the storylines of the American soaps. Books about the characters, faked local newspapers and maps of Ambridge (the fictitious village in middle England where the action is set) are starting to appear.

The text was transcribed from a two-minute, 20-second scene broadcast on 22 October, 23 October and again on 26 October 1986. I have screened out the paraverbal paraphernalia. This, of course, excludes the new and different meanings put into the 'original' written script by the actors. This is a limitation because of the non-correspondence between the transcript and the original. However, the scriptwriter may have spoken the original text into a Dictaphone with quite different intonation, and a complicated notation for emphasizes and pauses would not solve the problem; it would merely displace it.

The scene was not selected at random. I chose it because it illustrates some current concerns in the series which connect with those of its target audience. It also raises issues about social relations, in particular gender relations, in the non-soap world. Finally, it highlights a problem to do with interpretation – the interpretation we are permitted to construct of the 'real meaning' of a person's actions, and the interpretations social actors give of one another's acts. The distinction between a theoretical form of explanation and a lay form of explanation is one which is bound up with power. The distinction gives leverage to some social actors in positions where they are permitted to have access to knowledge. For those in other social positions, lack of knowledge can have the effect of reducing them to silence.

An immediate problem is that the temptation to intervene and flesh out the context is almost too much to bear. As with all data collection, the researcher can undermine the supposed objectivity of the process by supplementing the data with personal knowledge ('It was like this, I was there!'). Perhaps I need only allude to the structural class relations that cast Clarrie as the wife of the son of a poor tenant farmer, and Pat as a member of the Archer family which runs the estate. Those who are outside the community of listeners will not know that Clarrie's own father works as a labourer for the Archer family. Would it be helpful to suggest that Pat's interest in organic farming also helps maintain her own marginal position within Ambridge culture? To give such information outright would destroy the integrity of the text, but perhaps to let a few extra clues slide in unnoticed would be more in keeping with the spirit of deconstruction.

Pat Archer has picked up Clarrie Grundy, and she is giving her a lift to do her shopping. The scene opens with the noise of the car.

Pat: Er, look, I can drop you in the middle of the town but the trouble is I'm going almost straight home. How long do you think you'll be?

Clarrie: Oh not to worry Pat thanks. I'm dead lucky to get a lift one way. I can take the bus back easy.

Pat: What, with all your shopping?

Clarrie: Well, Dad said to start walking and he'd see if he could come and pick me up. Oh poor Dad. He was in a terrible state last night. His friend Dixie's dead.

Pat: This is his friend in Canada?

Clarrie: Yeah that's right. He ain't seen him in over thirty years.

Pat: Oh well, maybe he can go to Holland for his holiday instead.

Clarrie: Oh he were getting so excited about going to Canada too. Oh it's such a shame.

Pat: Ah, is the supermarket alright for you?

Clarrie: Oh yeah, lovely thanks.

Pat: My friend Jilly lives behind the supermarket, and I'm just dropping by to pick up the scripts for the panto.

Clarrie: What panto?

Pat: The Ambridge Christmas panto. It's instead of a revue this year.

Clarrie: Ooh that's nice! Which one is it?

Pat: *Cinderella.*

Clarrie: Oh! My favourite!

Pat: The script's written by some friends of mine. The writers' group call it a work in progress.

Clarrie: Do they?

Pat: That's not to say it isn't finished. There's a beginning, a middle, and an end. Well, er, a sort of end anyway.

Clarrie:	I thought *Cinderella* always had the same ending. She lives happily ever after with Prince Charming don't she?
Pat:	Well not in the Ambridge Christmas revue she doesn't. Not exactly. We're doing a modern reworking of the story.
Clarrie:	Oh, that's nice.
Pat:	What we're out to challenge is the standard interpretation of the story. What the writers' group calls the tyranny of the finished text.
Clarrie:	Oh yeah.
Pat:	I mean. Why should the ugly sisters be ugly? Why can't they just be sisters? If they were brothers, they wouldn't be the ugly brothers would they?
Clarrie:	Oh I do like pantos though. They're somewhere to take the kids after Christmas. Oh, there were one in Felpersham a couple of years back.
Pat:	I'm going to have to do something about Prince Charming too. I didn't do away with him completely. In real life there's no such person as Prince Charming.
Clarrie:	Well who's Cinders going to fall in love with then?
Pat:	She doesn't have to fall in love with anyone. She's her own person. She can find fulfilment in her work.
Clarrie:	Clearing up for the ugly sisters!
Pat:	No. I had something a little more elevated in mind. Erm Clarrie, can you come to auditions in the village hall next week?

Explanation

What series of explanations is Pat giving to Clarrie, and how may we understand the role and status of those explanations? As the text proceeds Pat explains why she cannot wait for Clarrie to finish her shopping and run her home. She explains what the rewriting of the panto entails, and why. Note that her first series of explanations is concerned with warranting and action which has a primarily practical aspect (dropping Clarrie), while the second set is concerned with warranting the production of a symbolic representation – an expression (writing a script).

There are two interconnected points about the nature of the relationship here between Pat and Clarrie. The first is to do with the transition from the practical resources. She is driving her car in which Clarrie is the passenger, and so she is able to determine Clarrie's behaviour. This practical leverage, however, operates through the expressive meanings through which Clarrie can understand the relationship. Thus Clarrie projects her disadvantages (heavy shopping and a bus journey) back on to Pat (concern about Clarrie:

'not to worry Pat thanks') in a display of gratitude for the lift. Pat sticks with the practical topics (where Clarrie's Dad could go for his holiday), ignoring the emotional focus of Clarrie's description of her Dad's troubles and her own concern for them. Instead, Pat waits, and then determines the transition to a later discussion of the panto. Pat handles the bridging sequence from one realm to the other by explaining why the supermarket is convenient as a point to drop Clarrie off, what the script is about, and finally why the script is a 'modern reworking of the story'. Pat, then, carries over the control she has over practical resources into the expressive sphere.

The second point is to do with the relative status of the practical and the expressive orders. (It would be possible to deconstruct the opposition. We could argue that ostensibly expressive activities are really practical in that they determine relationships and, therefore, what is deemed to be practical.) For the purposes of the present analysis, we make no assumptions about the supposed relationship between the two spheres, preferring instead merely to use the distinction as a device to understand what is going on.

In the text, Pat is implicitly using the distinction to identify and reproduce her relationship with Clarrie. Pat is able to introduce the question of the script for the panto. Pat constructs an explanation of the contents of the script, and lures Clarrie into playing a part that is an (expressive) representation of (practical) life in Ambridge. We should understand the nature of this luring in both its real and metaphorical senses. In a real sense, as Pat's invitation to Clarrie (to 'come to auditions in the village hall') makes clear, the upshot of the conversation is that Clarrie should actually play a part in the panto. Prior to that, however, Pat draws Clarrie into a discussion of drudgery, subordination and fulfilment in which *Cinderella* becomes the metaphorical frame through which they both might understand the real world. Pat, then, controls the expressive sphere through which she hopes to change practical relations.

But what is Clarrie explaining to Pat? In this text Clarrie's explanations are responses to Pat's topics (practical questions of where to drop Clarrie, and expressive constructions around the contents of the panto). Clarrie explains how she might cope with the shopping (Dad would 'see if he could come and pick me up'), and why Dad is in a terrible state ('His friend Dixie's dead' and he was 'so excited about going to Canada too'). There is also a level of implicit explanation where Clarrie attempts to express her view that the 'modern reworking' of *Cinderella* is not actually a real panto ('Oh I do like pantos though'), and that 'fulfilment in her work' would not be an escape from drudgery ('Clearing up for the ugly sisters!'). Note that, for Clarrie, explanation is a function of her acquiescence in Pat's explanations. She has little power. With these issues raised, we can turn to the elaboration of the deconstructive polarities which operate as a kind of conceptual cartilage for the text.

Deconstruction

Step one. Here there are two characters upon whom the conceptual polarities can be mapped. You might like to think of the opposing poles as being the dominant points in a definition of the situation in which the antonyms are suppressed and to which Clarrie submits. I can identify three oppositions: metanarrative/narrative, recasting/casting and reflection/subjectivity. Each pair raises issues about what social actors may understand about the relationship between what they take to be practical concerns and what they imagine to be the expressive gloss through which they represent those practices to others.

The recasting Pat engages in is one which attempts to break Clarrie out of her everyday role. As the conversation proceeds Clarrie gets drawn into a symbolic representation of her life, which is the script of *Cinderella*. The story parallels her own predicaments, but now Pat is raising the possibility that the story does not always have 'the same ending' (it is 'a work in progress'). The casting which stands in opposition to this is Clarrie's everyday role as dutiful daughter (with 'poor Dad') and harassed mother (where the panto is 'somewhere to take the kids after Christmas'). Clarrie refers to these aspects of the way she is cast in her life in Ambridge, but Pat resorts to inviting her to an audition which will radically recast her.

Clarrie's life, then, is being mirrored. An image is being wrought which is reflecting the character Clarrie plays in Ambridge. 'Look', says Pat to Clarrie at the opening of a text in which Clarrie is progressively reduced to silence. Her assertions about her own experiences (of 'fulfilment' equated with 'clearing up') – her own subjectivity – are discounted as Pat breaks beyond her social world ('the tyranny of the finished text') to write another for her.

Step two. Take the third polarity – reflection/subjectivity – first. How might Clarrie's view of her life be restored? More to the point, what attention might be drawn to the subjective investment Pat has in the mirror she holds up to Clarrie to recognize herself anew? Pat's control of resources, both practical and expressive, is at issue here, as is her power. Note the way that Pat's own subjectivity, her own involvement and responsibilities, are side-stepped by her when she defers to the writers' group statement about 'the tyranny of the finished text'. Does not the mirror she holds reflect herself, and does not the relationship between herself and Clarrie (Pat as holder of the mirror and Clarrie as the reflected subject) reproduced the relationship between the writers' group and herself (the writers' group as interpreters of the text and Pat as the relay of that interpretation)? The mirror, then, is also an expression of subjectivity.

By the same token, Pat is engaged in an activity where the recasting of Clarrie simultaneously enacts the casting of herself in the role of producer, director and purveyor of knowledge. Could we provoke recognition of the supposed recasting as a mere reproduction of the way Pat and Clarrie are cast as actors in Ambridge (with all the power that attends the unequal distribution of knowledge)? And again, the metanarrative to which Pat appeals functions as such only because it is a narrative invested with power – power Pat enjoys as a result of her knowledge of theory.

The next step. The third step of a deconstruction involves moral/political choices. These are choices which can only be pursued by the social actors themselves. There are issues about Pat's employment of theory to shatter Clarrie's everyday explanations, and how her use of that theory frustrates her desire that Clarrie should take control of her own life. These issues, of course, are to do with the relationship between power and knowledge. To offer prescriptions to our subjects recast as naive lay folk who might be enlightened by theory and liberated from the tyranny of the finished text would surely tangle us in the same contradictions.

Advantages and disadvantages

I will have to set my discussion of the advantages and disadvantages of deconstruction in the context of two separate, though related, discourses. One is the discourse of 'analyses of everyday explanation'. The other is the discourse of politics.

As with the structuralist strands of new paradigm social psychology, deconstruction locates conceptual categories which organize the text. Rather than posit these as being underneath what is said in the deep structure of interaction or in cognitive templates located in the heads of individual speakers, deconstruction finds these conceptual categories in the surface of the text itself. It recognizes that the categories are important because of the way they are used. Oppositions are the contradictions utilized by the speakers in their rhetoric to interpret and determine the actions of others. We saw this in the way Pat interpreted Clarrie's explanations within her own metanarrative as she tried to reflect Clarrie's life and recast her in a rewriting of *Cinderella*. More than this, a deconstruction also shows how the oppositions are contradictions which capture all subjects in a text and undermine the intentions of the authors of statements. We saw this in the way the power Pat wielded undermined her attempt to empower Clarrie.

As with the hermeneutic stands of new paradigm social psychology, deconstruction attends to the fluidity of meaning in a text. Instead of attributing this indeterminacy to the free exercise and expression of individual human intention, however, deconstruction locates the shifts of meaning in the text itself. Again, this focuses attention on the powers distributed to social actors in different positions. Power and language are intimately linked. It supports social actors' attempts to change power relations and to engage in the overthrow of dominant ideas. So we saw how it is possible to reinterpret Pat's mirroring of Clarrie's life and her attempt to recast her accounts in a metanarrative. Pat's rhetoric depends on the very issues of subjectivity, casting and narrative which she sought to exclude.

Deconstruction goes even further when it puts into question notions of everyday explanation. Theory itself is derived from ordinary explanation and is conveyed in a medium which uses the language of the surrounding culture. Then the theories seep back into everyday usage. Even complex debates find expression in the apparatus of everyday explanations and practically deconstruct the distinction between the two realms.

While the overthrow and transcendence of conceptual oppositions in the third step of a deconstruction is possible in philosophical and literary texts, a deconstruction applied to social texts raises questions of practical political involvement of the researcher in power relations. The first two steps uncover these relations, but the next step can only be taken outside the text. Without this step, which involves the construction of non-oppressive social relations, the hierarchies will simply be written and rewritten in the same old way. Listeners to *The Archers* will know that Pat's panto was abandoned, and the inhabitants of Ambridge returned to the Christmas revue.

A lesson which proponents of the new paradigm in social psychology tried to teach those gripped by the old paradigm was that a researcher had to go beyond data to ask people what they were doing. The process of gathering accounts is part of research and is the foundation of the idea that results are provisional and open to revision. While the fruits of a deconstruction are always ready for the next interpreter to get their teeth into, we are limited by the boundaries of the text. The sequences of signs which are offered to the reader are still there to be manipulated and pulled apart.

Social psychology in the new paradigm took what people said seriously, acting on the slogan 'treat people as if they were human beings'. Deconstruction, on the other hand, carries with it the danger of reducing persons to ciphers of the text. The relationship between knowledge and power, the violence which attends the prioritization of some concepts over others, also deeply affects the relationship between researcher and subjects. The theories in and around deconstruction also find their way into everyday explanation. The conflicts between Pat and Clarrie illustrate the problems of power which attend it. So when Pat is given a book by Lacan for her birthday this thrills the cognoscenti and drives back the inhabitants of the realms of everyday explanation (people like Clarrie) further beyond the pale of theory. The reading should be aware of the privilege that the position confers. The tyranny of the finished text can also operate when theoretically aware researchers approach and interpret the accounts given by the lay public. Perhaps this problem would be mitigated if proponents of deconstruction could advance a moral/political position. Both strands of the new paradigm in social psychology do propose a politics which flows from the value attached to a person's right to account for themselves and their actions. Unfortunately, in the case of deconstruction this is not possible without supplementing the approach. By its very nature it is hostile to any attempt to construct conceptual or political priorities. Further, I would want to resist the implication that Clarrie's resistance to Pat is somehow progressive. The reflection of social actors' lives and the recasting of their acts within wider political narratives is, I think, a 'good thing'.

I avoided confronting the issue of where the theory leads, and the power of theory in general, by choosing a text in which the speakers were no more than constructions. We may learn lessons about social relationships from such texts, but the pity is that a deconstruction would not necessarily lead to a progressive type of action research if it was applied to real explanations given by real people. I recommend that readers wishing to adopt deconstruction as a method take as their texts other fictions: discussions extracted from the pages of novels, or the products of role-play studies, or social psychology textbooks.

4 Constructions, reconstructions and deconstructions of mental health

This chapter explores the role of language and culture in our understanding of normality and abnormality, and uses deconstructive arguments to shift focus from psychopathology to discursive constructions that can be analysed in the qualitative research tradition. When we approach the concept of 'mental health' there is, of course, always a question about what this 'mental health' is that we intend to examine. These two words 'mental health' might, we think, be preferable to the couplet 'mental illness'; but, tempted as we might be to find some neutral terminology to approach this crucial research question, we know as qualitative researchers that every word we use is rich with meanings that will always locate words in discourses we may not want to endorse.

Contemporary discourse is replete with words and images that locate the causes for our activities inside individual minds; we increasingly inhabit a 'psychological culture' that delimits the horizons of our inquiry, and so the construction, reconstruction and deconstruction of those horizons of what is thinkable are what I am concerned with in this chapter. Here I illustrate my argument with examples designed to evoke what we might call 'mental health' as a cultural practice. That means being specific about the cultural examples, and I will show how this cultural specificity also bears upon the kinds of methodology we use to study mental health.

I take my examples from Finland – with a specific focus on the city of Tampere – and Finnish culture, which does abound with certain specific images of 'mental health', and I will make clear that my exploration of cultural images is conducted from the standpoint of someone working in Manchester – a peculiar post-industrial twin for Tampere. In this way we will produce some new reference points for deconstructing images of mental distress.

Whatever 'it' – this 'mental health' – is, it is a cultural practice, and to explore this cultural practice qualitatively there are some key requirements, and these are already methodological requirements.

Particularity of context

The first is particularity of context. Cultural practice is always something specific, even in conditions of rapid globalization that appears to suffocate local traditions. It is necessary to attend to this process of globalization as always also 'glocalization' in which local particularities of context are shattered and recomposed, deconstructed and reconstructed (Robertson, 1995). One only has to think of the phenomenon of 'world music' to see how local practices are abstracted and repackaged as part of the process of commodification for an international market.

Whatever might emerge as a 'transcultural' field of world mental health, then, will always have to manage the particular ways in which people from different parts of the world are classified and experience peculiar simultaneously normalized and pathologized emotional conditions of life. So, for example, we know that there are historical semiotic links between Tampere and Manchester. There have been some similarities of industrial development, and Tampere is sometimes referred to as the Manchester of the North, or 'Manse'. This is then apparent in the term for a form of Finnish rock music known as 'manserock'.

There are a few Finnish families in Manchester, and until quite recently there was a Finnish-language school. This transcultural aspect of contemporary life even has consequences for what the BBC represents as good mental health. Anna, according to one BBC Video Nation report, says that 'some of the scenery and buildings of the city centre [in Manchester] remind her of Tampere so much she hardly ever feels homesick'. The report continues: 'All she has to do is take a walk around Castlefield with her husband Matti' (Alajoki, 2003).

The deep cultural connections between Finnish and English culture are also useful here as an opportunity to draw attention to other cultural components that also connect with specific references to emotional states of well-being and un-ease, if not dis-ease. The Moomins, characters invented by the Finnish author Tove Jansson, first appeared in the London *Evening News* in 1954. I remember as a child being puzzled by the rather strange, depressive figures that appeared in the books about Moominvalley. The Hattifatteners, for example, are rather dangerous beings that travel in groups, with their only apparent goal being to reach the horizon (which is an issue that will also be of relevance for us here). Already, you see, there is cultural differentiation at work around what we imagine mental health to be. There is a permanent Moominvalley exhibition at the Tampere Art Museum, open every day, and there is a museum shop. Everything in the capitalist world can be commodified, including our fantasies and emotions.

You could say that these figures from Moominworld function in some way as representations of emotional states; we are able to attend to them, acknowledge them, but still keep them at a safe distance. The representation of something disturbing to us can actually be comforting if we can perhaps contain it. You will notice here that the way I am framing this relationship to disturbing things is quite therapeutic, and I will reflect on the prevalence of therapeutic discourse later on.

Particularity of focus

The second requirement is particularity of focus. Here we must address some problematic issues in qualitative research.

Some versions of discourse analysis focus on the actual things that appear in a text, and will refuse to go beyond that (see e.g. Potter, 1998). So, for example, if 'power' is not spoken about in a text, then it would not be legitimate to speak about power in the analysis. This approach is actually very English, and in line with a long-standing tradition of English empiricism; it is a tradition of research in which only things that can actually be observed are taken seriously. This discursive research is thus a form of 'textual empiricism'. It is quite well suited to a quantitative research paradigm, of course, but it is very problematic when it starts to stipulate what should be spoken about in qualitative research. When we are concerned with issues of mental health it becomes even more problematic.

This is a lesson that we can draw from the work of Michel Foucault, for in his history of madness, he emphasizes that his study is about particular kinds of 'dividing practices' that separate reason from madness (Foucault, 1961/2009). His is an account which circumscribes the shape of madness by tracing what reasonable discourse has to say about it. His account is thus formulating a boundary between reason and madness, showing us how something other than reason operates, operates as an empty space, a silence that itself defines what it is we fill with speech.

Some versions of discourse analysis also try to locate themselves within the accepted boundaries of social-scientific practice by adhering to quantitative research concerns with sampling and with kinds of 'data' that can claim to be representative. In that kind of research the assumption is that the larger the number of instances there are of a particular phenomenon the more confident we can be that we have found something worthwhile. The problem, however, is not only that a collection of instances drowns out the specificity of a case that is being analysed, but also that this approach prioritizes what is 'evident'.

There are more fruitful alternatives to this that are more congruent with the work of Foucault and with the general tenor of deconstructive analyses of cultural forms. Roland Barthes' (1957/1973) classic semiological analysis of the figure of the black soldier saluting the French flag on the cover of *Paris Match*, for example, had to conjure up the network of significations that operate as the condition of possibility for this image. We now recognize from feminist anti-racist work in qualitative research that we need to attend to the way that the pathologized presence of certain representations of a category of subject goes alongside normalized absence of certain representations (Phoenix, 1994). Notice, for example, that we do not actually see the French flag in the text Barthes analyses, and we certainly do not see the whole of the French occupation of Algeria in this image. It operates, instead, as a 'telling case' that we must decode and locate, deconstruct and reconstruct (see Stanley and Wise, 1983).

What is hidden from view may actually be more important, a more telling case, than what is evident. This is surely the way that ideological practices work to enforce certain kinds of normality and to pathologize certain kinds of experience; to make it invisible. The feminist movement, for example, developed out of activities of 'consciousness-raising' which brought into public discussion a multitude of experiences that had been hidden from view. In that process, what was brought into consciousness was reconstituted; certain conditions of possibility for speaking about experience transformed the experience itself. The speaking subject that emerges is always already positioned in relation to existing dominant categories of subject.

Particularity of history

In addition to these two methodological requirements – particularity of context and particularity of focus – there is a third methodological requirement, which is particularity of history, or, we could say, 'temporal particularity'.

If we turn again to Foucault's work we can see that the careful historical reconstruction of who we have come to be now is only possible because the kinds of questions we ask are questions about how to develop a 'history of the present' (Blackman, 1994). This history is a history of the changing boundaries that divide what is accepted from what has been excluded. So, in qualitative research that draws on Foucault's work, the focus on certain telling cases is a way of exploring a whole domain of discourse, and thus providing an analysis of how that discourse functions to constitute not only what we can immediately see as a number of countable instances, but what we cannot see and what only appears momentarily at certain points (Parker, 2005).

You might imagine that each telling case operates as an item in a projective test. Foucault was actually quite interested in projective tests, and administered Rorschach blot images to patients when he was working as a clinical and forensic psychologist, though this was years before he moved on to write about the history of madness and then genealogies of other concepts (Parker, 1995). Take the set of items from what has come to be a distinctively Finnish projective test, 'Wartegg'. (For a general overview of Wartegg in the context of projective tests see, for example, Cohen de Lara-Kroon (n.d.). The Wartegg items can be found at http://public.wsu. edu/~converse/wartegg.html (accessed 17 February 2014).) Many people, including students to be selected to study psychology, are given this test in Finland. The subject must doodle in the squares, and what they draw can be analysed; and there are other variables taken into account, which include the order in which they choose to fill in the different squares. Some items are included to make the subject feel anxious; one square with a little black square dot in it was designed to elicit anxiety, and so the interpretation will rest not only on what the subject draws but also how many other items they will prefer to fill in before they turn to tackle that one.

There is a crucial difference between a projective test and the analysis of discursive practice; however, in our analyses we examine how the categories that are used to produce a definable object that lies within reasonable discourse have been produced and how these categories function. Once again, this is a quite different notion of discourse to that which has become acceptable in the empiricist tradition. Discourse is not a massive observable corpus of statements, but it operates through certain potent signs, words and images which crystallize and speak of what is not spoken everywhere else.

Conceptual moves

We need to make two conceptual moves if we are to develop the qualitative research tradition further in order to tackle representations of mental health.

Attend to the boundaries

The first is to direct qualitative research not on 'mental health' as such but on the boundary that divides health from illness, normality from abnormality, reason from unreason. I use a number of oppositions here as if they are synonymous, as if they neatly map onto each other. Of course they do not. The question that we ask when we attend to the boundary is precisely what it is that is constituted on our side of the boundary – within the discourse we are able to use to speak about it – and what is produced as the disturbing, unsettling, frightening stuff on the other side of the boundary.

However, this kind of inquiry also needs to embed the analysis in relations of power and relations of ideology. The history of 'madness', to use a shorthand term just for a moment, is also a history of other relationships between the powerful and the powerless. The semiotic stuff and material practices that divide reason from unreason have always drawn upon, mobilized and transformed a range of other axes of domination and oppression. Path-breaking though Foucault's work on madness, discipline and confession has been, he did not adequately address the ways that class, culture and sex were always implicated in the construction of what we take to be 'normal' and 'abnormal' (Sawacki, 1991).

To bring those other axes of oppression into the analysis is not to weaken or dilute it, but actually strengthens the analysis we can then provide of the way 'mental health' operates across the fabric of society. Then we can see how mental health operates across the boundaries that simultaneously separate and constitute different categories of subject. One set of discussions around this kind of analysis comes from within feminist research, and around the attempt to conceptualize 'intersectionality' (see, for example, Yuval-Davis, 2006). To rehearse the argument very briefly here: in Western culture, we can see how the intersection between pathology, class, culture and sex has tended to operate.

First, the working class has traditionally been seen as the brutish mass that was insufficiently individuated to be able to engage in sophisticated 'talking cures', and mob behaviour in which the masses had completely taken leave of their senses was feared by psychological theorists. Second, those outside the civilized world were represented in the colonialist imagination and then in orientalist imagery as closer to nature, barbarians who were more likely to be afflicted by a variety of exotic pathological conditions. Third, femininity has historically been associated with madness. One only has to think of the images of 'hysteria' that were contrasted with what people took to be the norm, which was good strong masculine reason.

Attend to boundary changes

Let us move on to the second conceptual move, which is to attend to how the boundaries change.

This is where I want to turn to specific 'telling cases' to illustrate how some important changes might be operating so we can think about what the consequences might be. I want to tease out boundary changes that have taken place quite recently and the way those boundary changes are necessarily implicated in different axes of domination and oppression beyond 'mental health'.

Animals. A matter of great concern in recent critical work in psychology has been over the way certain kinds of emotions are essentialized. That is, they are turned from culturally specific descriptive terms into things that researchers in the positivist tradition then imagine can be identified in each and every human being whatever culture they inhabit. Critical work on the social construction of emotion has been a very useful corrective to this positivist tradition (Harré, 1986). However, the process of essentializing emotions is not restricted to that tradition of research. The spread of therapeutic discourse in Western culture has actually been a more potent force in encouraging us to think that we can isolate and 'resonate' with certain emotions.

This has also entailed a reformatting of the boundary between human beings and animals, and there is here a new version of the cultural practice of anthropomorphizing. Treating animals as endowed with human motivations and emotions is not new in West European culture. There was a time when animals could be tried for various crimes and sentenced in courts of law (Evans, 1906/1987). However, what we are faced with now is something new, for animals can be represented as having emotions which we do not necessarily find threatening – far from it; now we might actually connect with those emotions after they have been distilled into quack remedies.

Incidentally, there was, at the beginning of the twentieth century, a sub-speciality of psychology called 'plant psychology'. One study of the psychological index and psychological abstracts uncovered many titles of articles concerned with plant behaviour and even the 'mental life of plants' (Crellin, 1992). Like the criminal trials of animals, such things are wiped away by history because they become unthinkable when new epistemological and ontological boundaries are installed in a culture.

The language of connection and resonance with emotions to describe a practice that will facilitate mental health is an intrinsic part of contemporary therapeutic discourse. This therapeutic ethos relies on the identification and mobilization of distinct emotional states, and those who refuse to acknowledge and value these states are liable to be treated as pathological in some way; defensive at the very least. Every such specification of mental health entails a specification of how mental pathology will be understood, and it is our task as qualitative researchers to trace how the boundaries between the normal and abnormal are constructed and warranted.

Emotions always cluster around the motif of gender, and alongside the essentializing of emotions in new age therapeutic remedies we find the essentializing of gender itself. However, now something has changed in the boundary between masculinity and femininity. I noted earlier that femininity has historically been associated with madness, and this was certainly the case at the end of the nineteenth century at the time of the birth of modern psychiatry and psychology (Ussher, 1991). Therapeutic discourse, however, requires a view of emotion as something positive, something to be embraced, instead of something to be shut away.

The assumption that it is healthy to be 'emotionally literate' has transformed femininity from being a threat into being an asset (Burman, 2006). And, correlatively, this assumption transforms masculinity from being something eminently reasonable, once privileged over femininity, into something that is now a liability. It is now men who are the problem in Western psychological culture. The boundaries that define mental health have thus changed, and the intersection between these boundaries and other kinds of boundary between different categories of subject, here feminine and masculine, have to be included in our analyses.

Samurai. A second telling case is to be found in something more specific, in the motif of the 'samurai sword' in images of madness in British culture. It is not widespread, and it is not discussed endlessly, but it is a sign which condenses a number of different elements that are at play in Western conceptions of reason and what we imagine is 'other' to reason.

I do not know how far this image resonates in other West European countries, but there is something emotionally charged in images of the samurai in Britain. It is part of a more general orientalizing of Japanese culture, and Japan functions often as a limit case culturally and in social research; it is simultaneously similar and different (Burman, 2007; Parker, 2008a). The images of the samurai connote a romanticized vision of the warrior, but it is far enough away for it not to function as a threat.

Before I turn to some specific instances where this imagery has been mobilized, it is worth noting that the semiotic linkage between this orientalist image of the warrior and some kind of madness has been present for some years in US culture, and so it has also already been present to the British public. A classic episode of *Star Trek*, 'The Naked Time', which was first screened in 1966, had the crew of the *Enterprise* infected by a strange virus that afflicted each one of them in distinctive ways. This narrative device reveals some deeper assumptions about personality traits and what categories of subject are likely to contain them. One of the nurses, for example, bursts into tears and declares her love for Mr Spock.

The key example here, though, is Mr Sulu, who starts racing around with a fencing sword. An apparently trivial point, well known to Trekkies, is that the writer of this episode 'originally planned to have Sulu wield a samurai sword, but George Takei [the actor] convinced him that a samurai sword was too "ethnically consistent" for a worldly 23rd-century officer, so it was replaced with a fencing sword' (Gamaliel, 2002). Here is an issue for semiologists, for we have at play an image that functions by virtue of its chain of associations, and by what was absent rather than by what was present in the image.

In recent years the samurai sword has bubbled into public consciousness in Britain as something associated with madness. Let us turn to some brief examples from news reports.

From November 2000, the headline runs 'Man "flipped" in pub attack' and the first line of the story reads: 'A Swindon man who brandished a two-foot-long Samurai sword in a Merseyside public house has been placed on probation for two years' (http://archive.thisiswiltshire.co.uk/2000/11/23/230910. html (accessed 5 June 2006)). The sword offence is described as 'bizarre' in the story, and the use of the signifier 'flipped' evokes a moment of madness.

From July 2001, the headline is 'Swordsman's mother defends son' and the first line of the story reads: 'The family of a schizophrenic man shot dead by police as he brandished a Samurai sword have denied he was a danger to the public' (http://news.bbc.co.uk/1/hi/uk/1441582.stm (accessed 17 February 2014)). In this case the police in Liverpool were already so certain that someone with a samurai sword was dangerous that he was shot dead.

From June 2002, we now have 'Samurai sword attacker freed' and the first line of the story reads: 'A man detained indefinitely after attacking 11 churchgoers with a samurai sword has been released after less than two years, it has emerged' (http://news.bbc.co.uk/1/hi/england/2073623.stm (accessed 17 February 2014)). This story reassures readers that 'Seventy per cent of schizophrenics respond to treatment for their condition and new drugs on the market are far more successful at treating the illness', and so the medical model is evoked to contain the outrage provoked by the story.

From March 2003, a story has the title 'Loud party sparks samurai threat' and the first line of the story reads: 'Driven up the wall by the racket from a St Valentine's party, a Spa man threatened his neighbour with a Samurai sword' (http://archive.thisisworcestershire.co.uk/2003/3/19/220797.html (accessed 5 June 2006)). The phrase 'driven up the wall' functions here to evoke something of the madness that must have led someone to use a samurai sword.

From September 2003, the headline runs 'Samurai sword killer is sent to mental hospital' and the first line of the story reads: 'The samurai sword killer of a hero political aide, who grew up in Daresbury, has been sent to a mental hospital indefinitely – but only a medium security institution' (http://archive.thisischeshire.co.uk/2003/9/9/164994.html (accessed 5 June 2006)). There is, perhaps, an implication here that it is the use of the samurai sword that demands more than a medium security institution.

From April 2004, we have 'Teenager admits killing father with Samurai swords' and the first line of the story reads: 'A teenager has admitted murdering his father by stabbing him repeatedly with two samurai swords' (http://scotlandtoday.scottishtv.co.uk/content/default.asp?page=s1_1_ 1&newsid+3344 (accessed 5 June 2006)). In this story the teenager is reported as saying that Satan had told him to carry out the attack.

From October 2005, we read 'Samurai sword used in town attack' and the first line of the story reads: 'A man in his 50s has escaped serious injury after being attacked by a man wielding a samurai type sword in County Down, police have said' (http://news.bbc.co.uk/1/hi/northern_ireland/4305068. stm (accessed 5 June 2006)). Notice here the telling phrase 'samurai type sword'.

From May 2006, the headline runs 'Man killed with samurai sword in drug feud' and the first line of the story reads: 'Police are hunting two men after a drug feud ended with the murder of a suspected dealer with a samurai sword' (http://www.theguardian.com/uk/2006/may/18/drugsandalcohol. martinwainwright (accessed 17 February 2014)). Here the 'drugs' references function as signifiers that serve to explain why such a bizarre thing might happen.

We should note here the reiteration of the link between madness and violence, as if it could be taken for granted that someone who carries out violent acts must be mentally disturbed and as if mental ill health necessarily entails that they will be dangerous. There is a semiotic link here with the 'diagnoses' that are routinely given of political opponents to prove that they are mentally unbalanced and so a threat to Western civilization (Immelman, 1999, 2003). Once again, you may also notice that we have a string of cases in these newspaper reports of masculinity run riot, and some orientalism mixed in for good measure in the motif of the samurai sword.

Orcs. Let us turn to a third example of what I hope will serve as another telling case.

It was once said that hell will freeze over before Finland wins the Eurovision Song Contest, and I do remember one contest in which the Finnish contestant Kojo got zero points. One story is that his song 'Nuku Pommiin' – which we could translate as 'sleep to bomb' – refers to sleeping too late. Urban legend in Finland has it that, on the day when the finals took place, he did indeed sleep too late and missed the contest. (I thank Teija Nissinen for this anecdote (pers. comm., 19 June 2006).) One history of Eurovision says that his was 'the worst-rated song in a final' (Eurovision Record Book, http://eurovision.tummiweb.com/main.html?page=voting (accessed 19 June 2006)). But on 20 May 2006, of course, the hard rock band Lordi had a frighteningly triumphant win (with what was then the highest score in Eurovision history). There had supposedly been attempts by Christian groups in Greece, mobilized through an anti-Lordi campaign called 'Hellenes', to exclude the band from the country. According to one account, then, Lordi are Satanists.

According to a Norwegian blog they are like the Orcs from Tolkien's *Lord of the Rings* (http://norwegianthinker.blogspot.co.uk/2006/05/mordor-song-contest.html, accessed 19 February 2014). There has even been discussion of this in the English press, including the observation that if the contest was to be held in Mordor there would be a danger that the Shire and Rivendell would automatically award each other twelve points. You see the way chains of signifiers operate to link together quite different fields of culture.

The discourse circulating around Lordi is relevant to our discussion here precisely because of the way it marks a distinction between public and private, and between what is a performance on the one hand, and a rational individual subject who lies behind the mask on the other. There has been much speculation about why the band will not take off their masks, so it would seem that there is an absolute identity between the surface 'madness', as we might say, and the rational subject who is merely playing at being demonic. This would give space for psychological notions to be mobilized, and then it would make sense for the lead singer Mr Lordi to say, for example, in an article in the *New York Times* that 'In Finland we have no Eiffel Tower, few real famous artists, it is freezing cold and we suffer from low self-esteem' (Bilefsky, 2006).

This is a perfect opportunity, then, to recycle stereotypes about Finns, but you should notice here the role of a psychological variable, 'low self-esteem', for it is operating as a reassuring buffer-zone concept between us and pure evil, between us normal folk and unmitigated pathology. The coordinates of that formal opposition between the normal and the pathological can then be filled with a rich variety of ideological content depending on the particular context.

We have already explored how axes of gender, race and class become superimposed on the opposition between sanity and madness, but there are always a host of other culturally specific indicators that people have lost their minds. We only have to recall the panic about 'brainwashing' after the Korean War, and the fear that communists might exert some kind of thought control to manipulate people. The 2004 remake of the classic film *The Manchurian Candidate* is symptomatic here: originally made in 1962 but pulled from the cinemas after the Kennedy assassination, the film then starred Laurence Harvey, who was programmed by the Reds to shoot the US president. The mother was a communist agent who triggered the assassination attempt by showing her son an image he had been implanted with, which was the Queen of Diamonds playing card.

The remake of the film, made after the fall of the Berlin Wall, shifted to some vague conspiracy involving oil corporations in the Middle East, and so now the 2004 version is in line with a diffuse sense that big business is pulling the strings. There has been a significant cultural shift from the years of the Cold War, and this shift has consequences for representations of mental health. The coordinates of paranoia are always located in the most potent images of threat.

So, back to Lordi. In one Finnish cartoon a girl is asking her friend 'How will you recognize him?' and the other girl replies, as they turn the corner to meet a frightening Lordi figure, 'He said he will have a flower in his buttonhole' (which he does). The joke here is that Lordi are known to be really nice, sweet people. But the question remains, why don't they take off their masks? There have been rumours in Finland that the band members are KGB agents sent to Finland by Vladimir Putin to destabilize the country and so prepare the way for a Russian-led coup.

However, even this is a rather comforting layer of talk, and it is clearly part of the game, a part of the game in which fans collude with a performance knowing that it is just that, a performance. For example, after the band won the Eurovision contest there was discussion about what Tomi Putaansuu, the lead singer and former film student, really looked like; but when a magazine (*7 päivää*) did publish a photograph of Tomi without a mask, and two days later the other four band members were unmasked by another magazine (*Katso!*), a petition signed by over 130,000 people called for a boycott of the magazine in protest (and 130,000 out of a Finnish population of under five million is quite a lot).

The separation between public persona and the real person backstage was confirmed in newspaper reports; for example, in *The Guardian*, the report went like this: 'Scratching his nose with a plastic talon after his band's victory, Mr Lordi said,

In Finland, they've said things like we eat babies for Christmas. Whenever we appear in public people do their best to ignore us . . . We are not Satanists. We are not devil-worshippers. This is entertainment. Underneath [the mask] there's a boring normal guy, who walks the dogs, goes to the supermarket, watches DVDs, eats candies. You really don't want to see him.

(Booth and Smith, 2006: 3)

This is the giveaway. You don't want to see him because it would dispel the illusion, but the fact that it is an illusion is exactly what needs to be maintained. An 'illusion' signals that all is well, and there is certainly not a confusion between reason and what lies beyond, no delusion that would indicate that we have tipped into an abnormal realm from which there will be no escape (Parker, 2008b).

Construction etcetera

We have examined the construction of some images, but this still leaves some loose threads concerning reconstruction and deconstruction. As the historically constituted boundaries change around different constructions of mental health there is a continual process of reconstruction, and this means that we need to trace how that reconstruction happens and we need to have a particular kind of methodological stance towards that. This is where we come to the deconstruction of pathology (see Parker *et al.*, 1995; Parker, 1999b). What we accomplish in a deconstruction is simultaneously the production of something else. Let us return to Foucault for a moment. Reflecting on his studies of the dividing practices that constitute 'madness' as a certain kind of absence of 'reason', he says this, in an interview entitled 'Truth is in the Future':

I am not merely an historian. I am not a novelist. What I do is a kind of historical fiction. In a sense I know very well that what I do is not true . . . What I am trying to do is provoke an interference between our reality and the knowledge of our past history. If I succeed, this will have real effects in our present history. My hope is my books become true after they have been written – not before.

(Foucault, 1980a: 301)

We are now, then, diametrically opposed to an empiricist view of our objects of study, for we are now changing what it is we are examining, producing something new as we dismantle existing practices. A better way of putting it, though this admittedly is something that Foucault would not have been so happy with, is to say that we are 'dialectically opposed' to an empiricist view.

We need a different way of mapping 'mental health'. Maps of fantasy spaces can certainly be useful in freeing us from taken-for-granted assumptions about the world. However, the kind of map we need is one that will lead us from critical qualitative methodologies – the kind of semiological and genealogical studies that writers like Barthes and Foucault have been so useful for – towards a dialectical conception of research, which means that we do not merely interpret the world, but change it.

It is rather unfortunate that the Workers' Hall of Tampere is where Lenin met Stalin for the first time in 1905, and the approach I am advocating here is as much opposed to Stalinism as to contemporary neoliberal capitalist practice. However, as the website of the Tampere Lenin Museum, which is now the only permanent Lenin museum in the world, says, in a quote from Lenin, 'The decisive thing in Marxism is its revolutionary dialectic' (http://www.lenin.fi/uusi/uk/oikea1.htm, accessed 19 February 2014). Once again, the museum has a shop, for even Marxism can be commodified, and some very strange souvenirs are for sale, including some Lenin gloves which look as if they are designed for 'guerrilla gardening' (ecological activist interventions designed to question the built environment).

The revolutionary dialectic is a theoretical framework that is simultaneously directed at changing while interpreting. When we address questions of 'mental health' we are posed with the task of pairing deconstruction 'inside' psychology with deconstruction 'outside'. Dialectics here is not only a way of conceptualizing what the deconstruction might be aiming at but it also helps us to understand the relation between the two domains and the two forms of critical work as not merely complementary but precisely as dialectical, as interwoven and contradictory, and as historically interlaced and as open to change.

We need to be able to distance ourselves from the temptation either to insert a truly dialectical psychology inside the disciplinary apparatuses that makes up the domain of mental health or to romanticize a real human psychology outside in psychological culture. The deconstruction of mental health is thus not a nihilistic enterprise but it is actually more 'constructive' than approaches that are merely tangled up in the day-to-day reconstruction of the boundaries between the normal and the pathological, so tangled up in those changing boundaries that they fail to help us think that there could be anything different beyond those taken-for-granted cultural horizons. The task of radical qualitative research into mental health should be to tackle those boundaries and help open the way to something better.

5 Deconstruction and psychotherapy

This chapter connects the forms of 'deconstruction' we were working with inside psychology to a movement in psychotherapy that was also borrowing from the same kinds of ideas. The ideas had been developed as a 'narrative turn' inside systemic family therapy, and practitioners there had been able to develop a new practice in work that addressed the link between individual distress and social context. That work showed that deconstruction in psychology is not simply a new 'language game', and that there were powerful therapeutic consequences of taking Derrida's work seriously.

This chapter thus aims to take the 'narrative turn' in psychotherapy a step forward, and also include reflection on the role of psychotherapy in contemporary culture, drawing on the writings of Derrida and Foucault, and the development of critiques of language in psychotherapy that attend to the interweaving of meaning and power, and which together unravel attempts to reveal hidden personal truth. These critical perspectives also show how it is possible to find a place for reflection, resistance and agency to create a transformative therapeutic practice. These tasks are intertwined, and we find aspects of each of them teased through in different ways from different vantage points in this line of psychotherapeutic work.

The deconstructive approach in psychotherapy ranges across the various ways in which deconstruction can be used in psychotherapy as part of the process of exploring problems and 're-constructing' how they function in the stories people tell, in which deconstruction can be used as psychotherapy in the reworking of the relationship between therapist and client to address issues of power, and in which deconstruction can be developed from psychotherapy to reflect critically upon the role of this modern enterprise of 'helping' and expertise applied to the distress in people's lives.

The argument in this chapter needs to be located in the context of discursive and postmodern approaches (e.g. MacDonnell, 1986; Weedon, 1987; Doherty *et al.*, 1992). Although 'narrative', 'discursive' and 'postmodern' are often run together, as if they were equivalent or as if they led to the same kind of practice, I use them here to shift our attention away from narrative in the therapeutic encounter as such to include reflection on the way the therapeutic encounter itself is storied into being. I want to ask how psychotherapy is constructed moment by moment as people speak in certain ways *and* how the practice of psychotherapy is constructed as a kind of practice in which people believe they should speak like that (e.g. Siegfried, 1995; Pilgrim, 1997). An increasing attention to the range of narrative approaches in psychotherapy and the social construction of psychotherapy among practitioners and academics has provided the 'conditions of possibility' for these questions to be asked (e.g. McNamee and Gergen, 1992; McLeod, 1997; Monk *et al.*, 1997). To address these questions we move from the construction of therapeutic discourse to its *deconstruction*.

Deconstruction is an intensely critical mode of reading systems of meaning and unravelling the way these systems work as 'texts'. Texts lure the reader into taking certain notions for granted and privileging certain ways of being over others. Forms of psychotherapy which take their cue from psychiatric or psychological systems, whether these are behaviourist, cognitive or psychoanalytic, also take for granted descriptions of pathology which often oppress people as they pretend to help them. Deconstructive unravelling works through a kind of anti-method which resists a definition or prescription, for it is looking for how a 'problem' is produced the way it is rather than wanting to pin it down and say *this* is what it really is (Derrida, 1983). As we read any text, including texts about 'deconstruction', we look for the ways in which our understanding and room for movement is limited by the 'lines of force' operating in discourse, and this invitation to attend to the role of power in defining problems leads many critical readers to connect Derrida's (1980) comments on these limits with Foucault's (1980b) historical work. This also leads us to explore the way in which our own understanding of problems is *located* in discourse, and we must then reflect on how we make and may remake our lives through moral-political projects which are embedded in a sense of justice (Derrida, 1994) rather than given psychiatric diagnoses.

The conceptual apparatus of deconstruction in the theory and practice of psychotherapy is becoming increasingly popular among therapists working with 'problems' understood as narrative constructions rather than as properties of pathological personalities, and as embedded in discursive practices rather than flowing from developmental deficits (e.g. White, 1991; Lax, 1992; Parker, 1998a). It is also influential among a growing number of counsellors and helpers working in mental health support services generally who want to work with clients in ways that will facilitate challenges to oppression and processes of emancipation (e.g. White, 1991; McKenzie and Monk, 1997). Most of this work steps back from deconstructing the project of psychotherapy (e.g. White, 1991), but this step is one that is worth making. Here deconstruction is brought to bear on the key conceptual and pragmatic issues that therapists face, and the project of therapy is opened up to critical inquiry and reflection.

I will start with a brief review of the connections between deconstruction and psychotherapy. This is not with a view to dismantling psychotherapy so that it can then simply be 'reconstructed', but with the aim of developing an account of something different, a 'deconstructing psychotherapy' as a practice that is always *in process* rather than something fixed, a movement of reflexive critique rather than a stable set of techniques. I will sometimes use the term 're-constructing', but this is as a provisional tactic to help us move forward rather than a grand strategy to solve all the problems and close questioning down.

Sources and contexts

Deconstructive approaches lead us to therapy as a practice that is both respectful and critical. This double-sided process is complex and contradictory.

On the one hand, deconstructing psychotherapy is profoundly *respectful*. The therapeutic practices that are woven together in that therapeutic approach attempt to do justice to the stories people tell about their distress, the experience they have of problems of living and the struggles they are already embarking upon when they first encounter a counsellor or psychotherapist. The task is to engage with a narrative that seems to all intents and purposes 'problem saturated' and to work *within* it (White, 1989a). Those working in this approach acknowledge the complexity of the narrative precisely so that the contradictions can be opened out and used to bring forth something different, some 'unique outcome' that was always hidden as a possibility but needed a particular kind of sustained reflection to find it sparkling in the undergrowth (White, 1991, 1995a).

Important here is an attention to *contradiction*, for as people struggle with and rework their problems and trace through the patterns they make in their accounts, they find themselves elaborating different, competing perspectives. These narrative perspectives are sometimes aligned so that they seem to lie side by side and fit together, but there is a tension as they try to make us see the world in different ways at one and the same time. There is always, at least, a kind of narrative at work which takes up one kind of perspective that works from the standpoint of the problem and that is intent on holding the person in its grip. And against this it is always possible to find another narrative which takes up a perspective that flows from the standpoint of the person who is always trying to find ways of shaking the problem and perhaps escaping from it altogether. To be 'respectful', then, does not mean abandoning a standpoint, but it does mean acknowledging where we stand (Riikonen and Smith, 1997; Winslade *et al.*, 1997).

On the other hand, deconstructing psychotherapy is intensely *critical*. Therapeutic practices are embedded in images of the self and others that systematically mislead us as to the nature of problems. Deconstruction in therapy does not presuppose a self under the surface, and a deconstruction of therapy alerts us to the way such a notion of the self can unwittingly be smuggled in as some people 'help' others. Narratives of mental distress can all too quickly lock us back into the problem at the very moment that we think we have found a way out. So, the task of the deconstructing therapist, and just as much so the deconstructing client, is to locate the problem in certain cultural practices, and comprehend the role of patterns of power in setting out positions for people which serve to reinforce the idea that they can do nothing about it themselves (Madigan, 1992; Allen, 1993). In this respect, of course, there is a close connection with the kind of work which has been developed by feminist therapists (Seu and Heenan, 1998).

There is also an attention to contradiction here, and it is only by working through the spaces of resistance opened out by competing accounts and alternative practices that it is possible to find a lever for change. We are always already embedded in a particular set of perspectives, operating from within certain positions when we try to understand ourselves and others. To be 'critical', then, does not mean finding the correct standpoint, but it means understanding how we come to stand where we are (e.g. Griffith and Griffith, 1992). This is where a concern with justice in therapy becomes intertwined with a concern for social justice in the world that has made therapy necessary. Critical movements in the deconstruction of power in therapy are also engaged in opening up their work to the broader sociopolitical realm (e.g. Chasin and Herzig, 1994).

Dialectics and deconstruction: the personal and the political

We could say that the tensions that make 'respectful' work in deconstructing psychotherapy possible and which allow us to create something better in a narrative which is not problem saturated, and the tensions that make 'critical' work possible and make it possible to understand how we have been able to move from one narrative to another, are 'dialectical'. And the relationship between being respectful and being critical is also dialectical. These are dialectical relationships because they are contradictory and necessarily interrelated. The threads are knotted together in the picture we have of the problem and our practice such that they only take the tangled shape they do because they exist *together*, around each other. They exist as a 'unity of opposites', and they are played out in individual lives through certain idiosyncratic themes in a dynamic 'strategy of tension'. Like the disturbing interplay of dialogue and violence that pervades much contemporary politics, this strategy of tension is both the very condition for us being able to move in one direction or another in our relationships with each other in times of peace and, at moments in all our lives, it is the setting for a terrorizing arena of seemingly unending painful interpersonal conflict.

The advantage of this dialectical metaphor is that it connects the personal and the political. The development of this current of work raises once again the possibility, oft dreamt about in the feminist and socialist movements, of an approach to *individual* and *social* distress which links the two, and a view of relationships which understands the personal as political without reducing one to the other (Rowbotham *et al.*, 1979/2013). The search for a connection between these two spheres has led many psychotherapists from work with individual clients to an engagement with social structural problems, and it has also led many political activists into the realm of therapy to trace the ways oppression is reconfigured and reproduced at a personal level.

However, the problem with the 'dialectical' metaphor is twofold. It can threaten to leave us with a detailed description of a complicated interrelationship with no practical suggestion for a way out. This has been the limitation of approaches from within Marxism that have attempted to engage with psychotherapy (e.g. Cohen, 1986), and practitioners in this theoretical tradition have often, as a result, been very suspicious of the whole enterprise of therapeutic professionalism (e.g. Pilgrim, 1992). The dialectical metaphor can also lead us to the comforting and paralysing thought that there is nothing we can do now, but that we will one day be able to trace our way through to the synthesis of the oppositions and resolve the contradictions.

In this account, we would have to wait until a profound change in the social order, for a revolution, before we would be able to move from a description of the structure of the problem to its resolution.

But we cannot wait, and those working at the intersection of deconstruction and psychotherapy (and of course this intersection itself could be understood dialectically) are taking us through a way of working with the personal and the political which carries some of the force of socialist feminist visions of personal political activity which is always already 'prefigurative'; it anticipates forms of emancipated living that we hope to experience in the future, even after 'the revolution' perhaps, in the way we conduct our struggle to arrive there, the way we live now (Rowbotham *et al.*, 1979/2013). An assumption underpinning this 'prefigurative politics' is that we will never anyway be able to arrive at something better unless the means we employ are consonant with the ends we desire.

Perhaps the metaphor of 'deconstruction' is more apposite here then. That is the wager of those working with deconstruction in psychotherapy, and for most of its practitioners it invites a connection between the political and the personal which is *more* radical and practical than approaches derived so far from dialectics (cf. Dreier, 1997; Newman and Holzman, 1997). There are affinities between dialectics and deconstruction (Ryan, 1982), and it may be possible to quilt them together into a Marxist feminist practical deconstruction which simultaneously respects and carries forward the series of critiques that have emerged from post-colonial writing (Spivak, 1990). But deconstruction also promises us something more liberating, something open enough to respect our personal experience of conflict and the contradictions that we live with as we either bend to oppression or try to break it.

So, how do we move between respect and critique, and how is deconstruction helpful in describing and unravelling this, and what should deconstructing psychotherapy look like? Well, there are different ways of telling the story about how we could answer these questions. This is not to say that we should plait the threads together to arrive at one place. We can find different stories about deconstruction and psychotherapy in different places, and those different stories lead us in different directions. The crossed paths of deconstruction and psychotherapy in two different institutional arenas, critical family therapy and critical psychology, will serve to highlight some common concerns.

Critical family therapy

The first path to deconstructing psychotherapy is in the broad field of family therapy. A sensitivity to the intentional and unintentional abuse of power in family therapy in the 1970s, and critical reflection on the unwillingness or inability of practitioners to address this issue, has led to an influential current of work which promises something new and genuinely transformative.

Here the central defining problematic was one of *communication*. There was a critical impetus in this work towards questions of culture which we find marked at quite an early stage in the work of Bateson (1972) and Laing (1964), for example. Patterns of communication and miscommunication in families function in such a way as to produce complex systems of 'double binds' and unbearable 'knots' which lead to certain members being identified as the ones with the pathology. A pathological system can survive very efficiently if it can persuade one of its members that they are responsible and they themselves contain the problem. Traditions of 'structural' family therapy, which encouraged experts to operate as the saviours who might analyse and change alliances within the family (Minuchin, 1974), and then 'systemic' family therapy, which employed forms of questioning to reveal and reconfigure pathology in the family (e.g. Selvini *et al.*, 1978; Cecchin *et al.*, 1993), still tended to operate at the level of the family. This was the case even for the most radical anti-psychiatric sectors of this tradition, and the family itself was pathologized by the therapist as thoroughly as the family had pathologized its index patient (Jacoby, 1975). There was a way out, but it meant taking a step up and a step back.

Meaning and power. First, the step up. The therapist had to be able to move up a level in their understanding of patterns of communication to see the family as part of a network of meanings. Families absorb and reproduce images of pathology that are present in the culture, and these images are held in place by patterns of meaning that are interlaced with patterns of power. The privilege that is given to certain terms in certain oppositions in patterns of meaning is something that had already been worried away at in literary theory and philosophy, particularly in the work of Derrida (e.g. 1967/1978, 1981). And so the model of 'text', of the family as a text that could be read and rewritten in the context of the wider culture, was an important resource. It is to Derrida, for good or ill, that we owe the term 'deconstruction'. A de-construction is a process of critical reading and unravelling of terms, loaded terms and tensions between terms that construct how we read our place in culture and in our families and in our relationships, and how we think about who we are and what it might be possible for us to be. And so the province of literary theory, in critical reflection on reading and writing, and philosophy, in critical reflection on thinking and being, can be laced together in a profoundly practical way (Epston and White, 1989; White and Epston, 1990).

But there is more to it than this, for these family therapists were not engaged in a mere literary or philosophical exercise. To become a practical deconstruction in process in psychotherapy in the service of challenging pathology and changing lives Derrida himself had to be read alongside writers who were concerned with systems of communication as being embedded in systems of power. We can find in Foucault's (1975/1979, 1976/1981) work, at this point, a way of reflecting on the uncanny similarity between analyses of 'double binds' and 'knots' in families and paralysing contradictory messages that traverse a culture, and position individuals within various discourses and discursive practices (Parker, 1989). At the level of the family we already had descriptions of the way that a 'schizophrenogenic' mother may simultaneously demand that her child show affection and then recoil at every embrace so that the child is attracted and repelled and so may be made mad (Bateson, 1972). Similarly, when we read Foucault (1976/1981) we find descriptions of the way Western culture contains apparatuses which incite us to speak about our dirty depths and immediately shame us for speaking thus. We confess and are disciplined, and so then many of us are subject to 'dividing practices' and forms of incarceration which confirm that we must all always be frightened of falling into the realms of the mad (Foucault, 1961/2009). Foucault also encourages a critical reflexive twist in this account so that we are able to understand better how 'madness' itself and 'bad mothers' who make madness are constructions which bewitch us into blaming the victims (Parker *et al.*, 1995). This theoretical framework is invaluable for helping us understand the apparatus of psychiatry and the power of the 'spy-chiatric gaze' (Madigan and Epston, 1995).

Narrative approaches to distress which emerged from systemic family therapy in the 1980s have been linked in a number of useful texts with wider 'postmodern' debates across the human sciences (e.g. McNamee and Gergen, 1992). These developments have enabled practitioners in the fields of psychotherapy and counselling to draw upon theories of discourse and power in order to construct new forms of helping (Monk *et al.*, 1997). The 'deconstruction' of the problem that the client presents has, in some of the variants of this approach, been the focus of therapeutic work (e.g. White, 1991). Some popular developments in narrative therapy have moved towards a 'solution-focused' approach to pre-empt the framing and reification of the issue of concern as a 'problem' (de Shazer, 1985). Here any talk about 'problems' is eschewed, and the therapist deconstructs the categories the client may employ to make it seem as if there is a problem (de Shazer, 1991). Other more radical strands of work have preferred to take the problem seriously and to treat the problem as the problem. Instead of trying to deconstruct it away by refusing to talk about it, these strands of work focus on how the 'problem' is constituted in networks of discourse and power that position the client as helpless and as believing that the problem lies inside them (Chang and Phillips, 1993; White, 1995a).

Reflexivity and responsibility. So, second, the step back. At this point many family therapists came to see that they themselves were part of the 'system'. An engagement with a family in distress, an analysis of their pathology, an attempt to change patterns of communication, were each and all implicated in a kind of relationship which would serve both to reproduce and to transform what was going on (Cecchin, 1992). Systems of one-way mirrors through which the family could be observed and reflected upon within the compass of the professional gaze hardly served to solve this problem. The position of the therapist as a reflexive critical participating actor had to be included in analysis, and so new practices of accountability started to be developed (White, 1995b).

These practices have included innovations such as the 'reflecting team', in which the therapist becomes the object of study (White, 1995c). They have encouraged an opening up of the professional psychiatric practice to make it visible (e.g. Pilkington and Fraser, 1992; Simblett, 1997). These practices have also led to reflections on the way issues of power and boundaries between client and therapist serve to warrant forms of professional abuse and mystification of 'experts' (e.g. Lobovits and Freeman, 1993). This then connects with debates about 'professionalization' and the way institutions which govern therapy protect the professionals under cover of a rhetoric of protecting patients (Mowbray, 1995; House and Totton, 1997). This stepping back has also, of necessity, required a reflection on the cultural assumptions that underpin the very task of 'psychotherapy', and the ways in which the therapist will always be reconstructing forms of pathology if they allow themselves to imagine that they are neutral, disinterested professionals, and if they do not engage in a process of deconstruction with the communities they are part of (e.g. Tamasese and Waldegrave, 1996).

Readings and writings are always located in institutions, and the location of family therapy as an institution which was marginal to psychiatry permitted a flowering of critical work. The kinds of questions that have emerged within this institution have been framed by a particular context. The critical impetus has been driven by an attempt to be more respectful. Instead of the index patient or the pathological family system being treated as an object of the gaze of the expert, these progressive tendencies within family therapy have located the family in culture and located themselves in the same culture in order to construct an emancipatory feminist socialist humanist practice. These are the stakes of 'social justice' initiatives in this work, and the attempt to connect what goes on in therapy with what goes on in the world (e.g. Waldegrave, 1990; Grieves, 1997). A critical stance has been crucial here, and it has been in the service of respect for the lived realities of clients.

Critical psychology

The discipline of psychology too has seen a progressive turn to narrative in the last thirty years. This has been manifested in a turn to language and then a turn to discourse which has shifted attention from what goes on inside people's heads to the way that the narrative positions they adopt constitutes them as 'having' certain psychological states (Gergen, 1985; Harré, 1986, Davies and Harré, 1990; Parker, 1997a). Psychologists are then able to recognize these states as being the things they can predict and control, and this then constitutes individuals as subjects of the wider apparatus of surveillance and regulation in Western culture that psychology feeds upon and operates within. Each and every phenomenon that psychology takes for granted and uses to normalize and pathologize people can be shown to socially constructed (Burr, 2003), and debates over what is 'real' now in critical psychology revolve around our understanding of the social context for the production of mental states rather than whether they are universal and essential (Parker, 1998b).

Context. Foucault's (1975/1979, 1976/1981) work has been valuable here in showing how the twin tendencies of discipline and confession lock people together in such a way that the discipline of psychology becomes seen as a necessity, and is then able to pose as a solution. Psychologists are encouraged to think that they are able to change things, but they are part of a dense network, the 'psy-complex'. This network comprises the theories and practices which locate thinking and feeling inside individuals (Ingleby, 1985; Rose, 1985). Psychologists systematically delude themselves about their power in this apparatus, and this makes it all the more difficult for them to develop a critical reflection on the role power plays in people's experience of distress and their fraught relationships with professionals who are trying to help them.

The hope of many students early in their career in psychology is that they will be able to 'help' people. This is well-meaning, but we need to be careful about where it might lead. Why? First because there is the hope that 'help' is something that can be dispensed, and all the more effectively if an expert knowledge can be employed. The language that is used to frame the positions of those who 'help' and those who are 'helped' is deceptive (Gronemeyer, 1992). Even the word 'empowerment' betrays something of the position of the expert who thinks that they have been able to move an enlightened step beyond 'helping' people but cannot give up the idea that it is possible to bend down to lift someone lesser than themselves up a step, to give them a little empowerment (cf. Bhavnani, 1990).

Second, the idea that psychology can be used to help people is naive because it rests on the belief that the discipline is a neutral collection of tools which can be taken to help people if they are used wisely, or, perhaps, in rare cases, to harm people if used with ill intent. Psychology itself plays a paradoxical, duplicitous role here, for it first encourages the idea that it is best placed to help people suffering from mental distress, and we find this idea peddled with most enthusiasm in the attempts of the discipline to colonize therapeutic work through 'counselling psychology' (Woolfe, 1985). It then systematically crushes the aspirations of the well-meaning student as it repeatedly positions them as the 'experimentor' or 'researcher' who does things to other people (Burman *et al.*, 1996a). The only way critical psychologists can tackle this problem is, as a first step at least, to read *themselves* into the problem.

Subjectivity. The role of subjectivity in critical psychology has come to the fore in the development of qualitative approaches (e.g. Banister *et al.*, 1994; Henwood and Parker, 1994). This has made it possible for some psychologists to turn around and reflect on the way they tell stories about people rather than pretend that they are 'discovering' facts about behaviour. The research process is then opened up to the activity of interpretation, and an increasing number of psychologists are then able to realize that an interpretation calls upon their own place in the phenomenon. They are then no longer distanced neutral observers, but part of what they are studying, taking responsibility for the sense they are making.

The turn to language and discourse in qualitative research has been profoundly influenced by feminism, for feminists attend to questions of power as they flow from the big political arenas through to our experience of our own position as gendered subjects and back again. There has been a growth of critical reflection on psychological practice as gendered and as structured by images of culture and class (e.g. Burman *et al.*, 1996b), and 'feminist psychology' itself has then been subject to critical reflection, to deconstruction (Burman, 1998). Critical psychology is then able to work with complex notions of power and subjectivity, and the link between social structural change and therapeutic work is then put on the agenda. This reflexive turn has thus been connected with the turn to discourse in the discipline, and they have together opened up a space for a reconsideration of the practice of psychotherapy (e.g. Hare-Mustin and Marecek, 1997).

The development of these critical tendencies in psychology has been conditioned by their institutional location. Just as critical family therapists were driven to ask certain questions about their practice because of the context they were working in, so critical psychologists have been profoundly affected by the way their discipline encourages them to think, and their particular arenas for resistance to those dominant practices. The attempt to find a way back to helping people and to respecting them has been through the development of critical work.

The emergence of deconstruction in different institutional locations has also served to remind us that 'deconstruction' is not a single thing, and cannot be summed up in a neat definition or be put to work as a discrete technique. Deconstruction is a form of questioning, a processual activity that defies definition, and it is marked by the very forms of *difference* that it theorizes (Derrida, 1983). Derrida (1994) has reminded us that deconstruction should not be reduced to simply talking about difference, and if we are to avoid getting bogged down in the quagmire of relativism in academic 'radical' psychology (e.g. Parker, 1998b) we also need to put deconstruction to work practically to really make a difference.

Conclusions

Ideas from the broad field of deconstruction have been used to support and extend the range of techniques in narrative therapy. Here 'deconstruction' appears in psychotherapy as a system of concepts that can be directly useful in conceptualizing what is going on and moving things forward (Madigan, 1992). We might even be tempted to think of these ideas as operating as discrete tactics, and indeed they are sometimes used in that way. They can appear as kinds of questioning and reframing, as the externalizing of problems (White, 1989b; Roth and Epston, 1996; Stacey, 1997) and internalizing of invisible friends (Epston, 1993). Here deconstruction itself is an invisible friend that has been taken into the process of psychotherapy and has assisted a progressive reworking of the encounter and the institution. Instead of simply reconstructing psychotherapy, however, and moving from the use of critical ideas to the improvement of therapeutic practice, important though that may be, we need to move in the other direction, and we need to keep our 're-construction' at work as a provisional tactical activity. Our social constructionist 're-construction' is then in the service of deconstructing the resources that are already starting to be sedimented in narrative therapies, externalizing those resources to make them visible.

6 Deconstructing diagnosis
Psychopathological practice

This chapter explores the process by which ordinary people are turned into objects by the discipline of psychology and related parts of the 'psy-complex'. With the increased power of the psy-complex we have seen a relentless psychologization of society and the proliferation of diagnoses of forms of unhappiness. The increasing popularity of psychotherapy and counselling is both a symptom of and a response to this process. As social problems become located more firmly inside individuals, each of us then experiences our distress as something which must be addressed as something intensely personal.

Perhaps this is not necessarily a bad thing, and we do need to be able to develop a response to social problems which works at the interface of the personal and the political instead of pretending that society is something separate from us. However, I argue in this chapter that while some of us may participate as clients or providers in psychological services with this progressive purpose in mind, we are always also faced with the more reactionary side of this process of psychologization, where forms of expert knowledge are used to identify psychopathology and so to specify what we should feel as normal or abnormal. This psychopathological practice, which increases distress at the very moment it defines it, finds its quintessential expression in the activity of diagnosis.

The chapter draws upon deconstruction to argue that the categorization of people within the *Diagnostic and Statistical Manual of Mental Disorders* is itself a form of psychopathology. That is, it turns around the opposition between those who carry out the diagnosis (professional psychiatrists or psychologists who claim to be using an objective diagnostic system) and those who are subjected to it (those positioned as the 'patients' or 'clients' who have the pathology identified within the diagnostic system).

Diagnosis transforms the varieties of ways in which we might achieve and enjoy mental health into a bewildering range of categories of dysfunction and mental illness. People living in varying degrees of discomfort or unhappiness are themselves transformed into categories, and modes of behaviour and thinking are then prescribed and proscribed for them. Prescription follows ineluctably from the diagnosis when certain expectations about what the patient should do, what they have done and what they might be expected to do in the future are elaborated. Proscription accompanies this normalizing of states of health and illness when certain experiences and feelings are consigned to the realm of illness. Until the early 1970s these included kinds of sexual orientation, and nowadays they still include the hearing of voices, for example. It would seem from social and psychiatric trends in North America that even mild states of depression that all of us sometimes experience will soon be suppressed with drugs. Diagnosis brings with it dehumanization, labelling, the pathologization of many human activities, and iatrogenesis (Illich, 1976). Here, the career path of those who have been subjected to the sometimes well-meaning attempts to comprehend exactly what they 'have' or what they 'are' often leads them into more profound distress as they undergo treatment or struggle to understand what professional logic governs the treatment.

Histories of the presenting problem

Diagnosis has become more prevalent as modern life becomes more complicated, and its practitioners have had to become more creative to counter the many attempts to shake them off. Diagnosticians are convinced that they can see exactly what is wrong with other people, or that one day they will be able to do this. They function as parasites upon the unhappy, dependent on the very complexity and mutability of the unhappiness that sustains and frustrates them. There have been many attempts to understand the way that the obsession with making diagnosis is itself a form of psychopathological practice, and what tormented certainties afflict the diagnosticians.

The anti-psychiatry movement in the 1960s, for example, was inspired by Laing's (1965) insistence that despite his medical and psychoanalytic training he could not agree that the person sitting with him in a session was a collection of symptoms. The removal of homosexuality from the *Diagnostic and Statistical Manual of Mental Disorders* (DSM) in the 1970s would not have been possible if the gay liberation movement had not refused to accept that they suffered from a condition that could and should be cured, and lesbian activists are still at the forefront of radical critiques of psychiatric reasoning (Kitzinger and Perkins, 1993). Feminists have challenged the ways in which diagnostic systems pathologize women's experience, and the rise of counselling and psychotherapy has, in part, been a result of the involvement of feminists in mental health practice as an alternative to psychiatry (Ussher, 1991). There have been many forms of resistance to the treatment of the experience of cultural minorities by white psychiatry, and this has entailed the rejection of approaches which reduce the person to a diagnostic type or to being an exemplar of a certain community marked by distinct exotic forms of pathology (Littlewood and Lipsedge, 1989).

There have always been alternatives to diagnosis. Within the broad domain of counselling and psychotherapy, systemic family therapists have always attempted to understand how the 'index' patient carries and expresses a collective pathology, and their implicit resistance to the diagnostic response of a family to conflict has become more explicit recently in the emergence of narrative therapies which see images of pathology as carried by kinds of discourse in the surrounding culture (Monk *et al.*, 1997). The Hearing Voices Network has emerged to challenge the way the hearing of voices is usually treated as if the voices were necessarily pathological 'auditory hallucinations' and so a first-rank symptom of schizophrenia, and it has been building supportive environments for coping with or celebrating voice-hearing instead of diagnosing it as a symptom of something else (Romme and Escher, 1993).

In some cases the very attempt to resist diagnosis is treated as a symptom which must be located in a diagnostic system, and each of these attempts to escape psychiatric reasoning has also succumbed at some point as some personnel trace a career path into counselling or psychotherapy and take it too seriously.

Deconstructing psychiatric power, and resistance

Each of these different movements employs a theoretical framework to make sense of diagnosis, to understand how diagnosticians come to believe that it works and to challenge the way it is implemented. A framework that has been particularly useful to us has been a form of 'practical deconstruction' which reverses the priority given to certain concepts, locates those concepts in certain relations of power and supports resistance on the part of those subjected to them (Parker *et al.*, 1995).

With respect to the first aspect, I have already been turning the form of reasoning that diagnosis employs against itself. Those who are so intent upon fixing pathology in others can themselves be 'diagnosed' as suffering from an obsession with order and with arranging people in a set of a categories (Lowson, 1994). The relationship between diagnoser and diagnosed can thus be reversed. However, this kind of simple reversal is only the first step in a deconstruction, and we then need to develop an analysis of the way 'diagnosis' operates independently of the wishes of any particular person, whether they be professional or client. Deconstruction as a particular form of conceptual analysis and theory of meaning has always been attentive to the way we try to find anchoring points where meanings seem to be 'present', self-sufficient and independent of context, and to the way this attempt to fix meanings unravels under a little pressure. To understand how meanings of symptoms appear to us as if they were signs of something else, as if they were the natural expression of diagnostic categories, we have to look at how the diagnostic texts, in the International Classification of Diseases (ICD) and DSM for example, have been structured.

The ability of diagnosticians to impose their own stereotypical distinctions on others is made possible by the wider systems of power that weave counselling, psychotherapy and psychology together as a dense network of theories and practices, termed by some critics the 'psy-complex' (Ingleby, 1985; Rose, 1985). At this point we need to go beyond simple 'deconstruction' as such – the kind of deconstruction one finds in much contemporary liberal literary theory – and locate diagnostic texts in the psy-complex. The psy-complex contains prescriptions and proscriptions for the behaviour of mental health professionals as much as it does for their clients, so that when a counsellor or psychotherapist rejects diagnosis they may face disapproval or even sanctions from disciplinary professional organizations (Mowbray, 1995; House and Totton, 1997).

A practical deconstruction is not satisfied with the academic game of juggling conceptual oppositions and identifying the ways they work in relations of power; rather, we should always look to forms of resistance. This is all the more necessary because resistance to diagnostic categories functions in such a way as to construct alternative moral-political communities, and these provide points of reference for people with problems to see that they may be able to live without their problems. The disciplinary side of the psy-complex which fixes people in their place and sees them as the source of distress is complemented by a confessional side in which each individual feels themself to contain that distress and believes that they will only find relief by speaking about it within certain acceptable forms of expert discourse (Parker, 1998a). Resistance may indeed include the right to speak about abusive or oppressive experiences and to work with others to develop a collective voice on such matters, but this means speaking out of turn and outside existing systems of categories. Examples of this resistance also provide evidence that diagnostic systems may not be necessary at all.

Diagnostic culture and its contradictions

Diagnostic systems are fragile things without systems of power to hold them in place. The underlying assumptions about cognition and emotion that must be made by diagnosticians for them to make sense are easily dissolved if we step back and look at them in cultural context. It would be a mistake to say that diagnostic systems like DSM and ICD are 'arbitrary', but they are certainly contingent on quite narrow local historical, cultural and sub-cultural conventions.

The sense of the self as an internal delimited entity coterminous with the physical duration of a body is wedded to common sense in Western culture, but it has not always been like this (Heelas and Lock, 1981). Seemingly fundamental emotions also seem to be quite recent, and other descriptions of emotion, in medieval England for example, simply do not make sense to us now. Other cultures are structured around different notions of 'self', if that should even be employed as the appropriate term for individuated experience in those contexts, and different patterns of emotion are made possible by different forms of description (Harré, 1986). If present-day Western assumptions about self and emotion have not always applied and do not apply around the world, then how can diagnosis proceed? It could be argued that these gross historical and cultural differences can be bracketed out, but this is a desperate and dangerous move for it must then either ignore the existence of people from different cultures – and this has tended to be the way in white psychiatry (Fernando, 1988) – or it introduces additional diagnostic procedures to identify special patterns of pathology in minority cultural groups – and this has tended to be the option favoured by psychiatrists interested in 'transcultural' approaches (Mercer, 1986). Either way, anyone different is pressed into a diagnostic system. The problem is worse than this in practice, however, for no culture is homogeneous. It is always fractured at least by age, class, ethnicity, gender and sexuality.

It has been within the contradictions between official and unofficial knowledge which are made possible by such fractures in society that alternative 'deconstructive' therapeutic practices have developed. We see this, for example, in the activities of 'deconstructive' or 'postmodern' narrative or discursive therapists who explore the way the 'problem' has become storied into being and internalized by the client (White, 1991). The 'externalizing' of the problem in this work is a profoundly anti-diagnostic process, reversing the ways in which a person has been made into the problem and helping them treat the problem as the problem, using deconstruction with and against psychotherapeutic power (Parker, 1999b).

Deconstruction of pathological practice is not simply a negative 'destructive' refusal of all that has been learnt by those labouring in the psy-complex. Counselling and psychotherapy which employs deconstructive analysis as part of the therapeutic process is in some ways a quite 'constructive' activity. What makes it so different is that this anti-diagnostic activity is constructed with the client as part of the process of emancipating the client from the problem (and they may then deconstruct the problem), and it must of necessity operate against the efforts of the diagnosticians who construct and implement the DSM or ICD in such a way as to subject the client to the problem (by which they then ruthlessly reconstruct the problem).

Diagnostic systems would, perhaps, be less dangerous if they rested on sound empirical foundations and if the allocation of individuals to the categories could be made smoothly and logically. Unfortunately, counsellors or psychotherapists who employ diagnosis are drawn into a system and process of application that has little foundation in reality and which mystifies those who attempt to make use of it. Studies of the contradictions and gaps in research on 'psychotic language', for example, have concluded that the discourse in which such impossible and untenable distinctions are made is itself 'psychotic' (Parker *et al.*, 1995). There is little agreement between observers of behaviour deemed to be pathological as to which categories are relevant. Psychiatric patients thus find themselves placed in a confused overlapping series of different categories, and confusion on the part of the psy-complex is then projected deeper into the patient as further confirmation of their pathology.

Tactics and ethics

This does not mean that it is not sometimes necessary to use diagnostic labels. In some settings we use a label to enable communication between professionals, and between professionals and clients. In other settings we may play with labels precisely to show how mutable they are.

When the psychiatric hospital of San Giovanni in the northern Italian city of Trieste was closed down as part of a wide-ranging reform of mental health provision in the 1980s, for example, personnel in the new community mental health centres had to continue using some of the ICD diagnostic categories (Ramon and Giannichedda, 1989). This was primarily because European Community funding was predicated on the existence of certain mental health problems and community provision for ex-patients, and returns had to be made to the project organizers about the prevalence of certain kinds of symptomatology among the users of the health centres. On the one hand, then, the ideology of the reforms was driven by an attempt to dissolve the distinction between the 'psychiatric' patients and the wider disparate community of the 'emarginated' (the homeless, the youth, the unemployed). On the other hand, if a homeless person were to apply for a bed for the night at a community 'mental health' centre, they would have to display a recognized diagnosable psychiatric complaint. It is in such a fashion that counsellors and psychotherapists often communicate with psychiatrists. Similar tactical moves have to be made by those who want to keep diagnosis intact but reframe it in terms of 'risk' and 'risk prediction'. Diagnostic categories can be useful to display the effects of racism, sexism and poverty on mental health, turning them against the very system that employs them. Even those using radical 'deconstructive' approaches may have to speak the same language as diagnosticians, but their task is to help their client speak many other languages as well as that one, and to be able to understand how that language as diagnostic discourse works to mislead them about what and where the problem is.

When members of the Hearing Voices Network participated in an academic conference on theories of voice-hearing in Manchester in 1994, the 'practical deconstruction' of diagnostic categories that this meeting invited entailed a deliberately excessive flood of diagnoses so that many different systems could be brought to bear on voice-hearing by voice-hearers themselves. Not only was this meeting a festival of explanations, then, but it was also a festival of diagnosis. Psychiatrists and psychologists were permitted to rehearse their categories and theories but now alongside speakers who explored shamanism, spiritualism and telepathy as diagnostic and anti-diagnostic tools. There have been many other initiatives of this kind since (Coleman, 1997).

In either case, however, those who use diagnosis are doing so tactically, and with a view to encouraging critical reflection on the categories and the procedures by users of services rather than luring us into the illusion that we are tapping some deep enduring truth about forms of psychopathology.

Diagnosis as psychopathology

Diagnosis is a crucial issue for counsellors and psychotherapists, for they are brought face to face with a moral-political choice about where their allegiance should lie. If we agree that diagnosis captures forms of underlying pathology, then we may well find ourselves on the side of the psy-complex and we will reproduce all the assumptions and relations of power that underpin it. This is dangerous on three counts.

First, hierarchies of expertise inside the psy-complex are reproduced. Diagnosis of any kind threatens to do this, for psychiatric systems – with the DSM and ICD as the key examples – define how other psychotherapists and counsellors categorize people, and so these professionals who are lower down on the diagnostic pecking order are themselves subject to a good deal of mystification as they implement elaborate abstract stereotypical judgements on the real people they are trying to work with. Often counsellors and therapists use diagnostic systems after thinking through why, and deciding that they are simply doing it for pragmatic tactical reasons, usually to please the bureaucrats who like official records organized around certain categories. The DSM and ICD can now be read simply as detailed descriptions of symptoms rather than a guide to the discovery of underlying disease states, and 'symptomatology' has even been posited as an alternative to diagnosis (Bentall, 1992). There are even quite a few psychiatrists involved in therapeutic work who know that the diagnostic categories are a post hoc representation of a problem, but the structure of power in the mental health system is such that they have a freer rein to voice their uncertainties about such matters. The worst cases are those psychiatrists and their hangers-on who are enthusiastic about diagnosis; for them it serves as a form of control, often to control their own anxiety about being in the presence of distress, and these people are as much a danger to themselves as to others.

Second, hierarchies of emotional ability are reproduced among the client population. Psychotherapists can sometimes be tempted to find security in alternative institutional or home-spun diagnostic categories, and these too can serve to fix people in place as firmly as do the DSM and ICD. Lacanians, for example, make a strict distinction between neurosis and psychosis and between hysteria and obsessional neurosis, and see diagnosis of these clinical structures as tapping something laid down very early in childhood and as not susceptible to change (Evans, 1996). A more widespread, softer, and for that more pernicious, diagnosis psychotherapists and counsellors are encouraged to make is as to the level of 'psychological-mindedness' and so the extent to which a client might be expected to engage with and benefit from therapeutic work (Coltart, 1988). Not only does this often smuggle assumptions about race and class into professional perceptions of those unsuitable for treatment, but it also prevents those diagnosed as 'schizophrenic' from receiving therapeutic support. Psychological-mindedness here is often assumed to include the client having a notion of an unconscious, something that many narrative therapists (for example) would not even sign up to.

Third, hierarchies of soft and hard truth are reproduced. We find ourselves on the slippery slope of deference to psychiatry and the illusion that there is a hidden hard truth under the soft stories we learn in our own counselling and psychotherapeutic practice. Not only is this mystifying, but it also legitimizes terrible abuses of power on the part of those who seem to be dealing with the hard stuff. Here the terrible practices of drug 'treatment' and ECT (Electro-Convulsive Therapy) await as options for people who are not deemed suitable subjects for therapeutic intervention (Coleman, 1998). Diagnosis gives warrant for these things too, practices which many counsellors and psychotherapists have devoted their lives to helping people to avoid as they help people to help themselves.

To refuse diagnosis is to take the side of the client and to challenge the relationship between those who think they know and those who are attempting to become experts on their own lives, and in the process we can deconstruct psychopathological practice.

7 Deconstruction, psychopathology and dialectics

With Derek Hook

This chapter includes another voice, that of Derek Hook, who took on an earlier version of a paper that I wrote for a conference in South Africa on psychopathology and which I submitted to an edited book afterwards. The editors of the book did not like the paper, but Derek worked on it and guided it to publication in the *South African Journal of Psychology* in 2002 (and so he was, of course, listed there as first author). The chapter takes as its focus 'psychopathology' and explores the connections between a 'deconstructive' critical analysis and a radical 'dialectical' analysis. The chapter resituates the diagnosis that is made of what is diagnosed by way of 'psychotic discourse'.

Our objective here was to critically engage with privileged notions of psychology on the reciprocal levels of the personal and the political, the subjective and the social. An additional tool that becomes important here, in linking the internal and external deconstructions of psychology, is dialectics (something I have linked deconstruction with in earlier chapters in this book). Dialectics is a means of comprehending the relation between different forms of critique and the relation between different domains in which the psychological is worked through.

Connecting the spheres of social relationships with individual activity, and the realms of political and personal in this way, enables a critical linking of the individual and the social without reducing one to the other. Engaged, albeit schematically, in this way, psychopathology may be approached as a construct that has been storied into being in psychiatric texts where it has been sedimented in practices which make it look and feel substantial and real. To critically engage with constructs of psychopathology, then, it is necessary to simultaneously grapple with the objective and subjective aspects of the problem.

This chapter is about deconstruction and its limits in relation to pathology; and about the way we can reconceptualize the relationship between 'the normal' and 'the pathological' in critical research. More directly, this chapter is a theoretical attempt to question how we might contest essentialized and reified concepts of psychology and psychopathology as they are represented and experienced in the broad domain of what we might refer to as 'psychological culture'. Given the centrality of psychopathology to psychology, the reconceptualization of this relationship is a key aspect of the broader project of 'critical psychology'.

This line of discussion requires a series of qualifications, however, and so before proceeding, it is important to specify what is meant by certain of the foregoing terms. First, in speaking of 'psychological culture', we are trying to evoke a sense of how psychology is broadly disseminated, how it circulates, functions in, and acts as a cultural resource in everyday, contemporary cultural life. This notion attempts to express the pervasiveness with which formal and informal accounts of psychology *inform* common sense. In speaking of psychological culture, we are, in short, speaking of popular culture as drenched in psychological talk. To get a grasp on psychological culture, to work on it with something able to exert a potentially transformative influence, we will to be able to engage with issues of subjectivity, and more than just this, with issues pertaining to *the fabrication of subjectivity.* In other words, we will not simply be approaching psychology, or psychological culture from a social vantage point – from how it is effectively and widely implemented in the world – we will also be looking at how psychology is implemented and operated from within the individual, so to speak, on the level of self-understanding and subjectivity (Butchart, 1997; Swartz, 1996).

Critical psychology, second, is that approach to psychology which examines how certain varieties of psychological action and experience operate ideologically and in the service of power (Parker, 1999a). More than this, critical psychology also studies how psychological culture operates beyond the boundaries of academic and professional practice. Furthermore, critical psychology entails also the investigation of how everyday activities might provide the basis for resistance to contemporary disciplinary practices (Gordo-López, 2000; Parker, 1999a).

Third, deconstruction, at a general level, is a way of destabilizing and uprooting those normal, given or common-sense notions that we typically rely upon to make sense of the world. More specifically, and as Parker and others have discussed elsewhere (Parker *et al.*, 1995; Parker 1999b), deconstruction is an intensely critical mode of reading systems of meaning, a means of unravelling the ways these systems work as texts. Following Norris (1996), 'to 'deconstruct' a text is to draw out conflicting logics of sense and implication, with the object of showing that the text never exactly means what it says or says what it means' (p. 7). The argument of Derrida, the foremost proponent of this approach, is that philosophy, like literature, and any broad system of knowledge and explanation, is a product of rhetorical figures and devices. Such systems of explanation – although Derrida (1967/1978) clearly has philosophy foremost in his mind – exhibit a reluctance to face their fundamentally rhetorical nature.

In this way, deconstruction provides a useful way for re-reading and reworking those ideas and practices normally taken for granted in everyday life. Within this chapter, we will be using the notion of deconstruction precisely to refer to the unravelling of hierarchies of concepts which structure how modes of being are represented, essentialized and experienced in psychological culture. Furthermore, it is important that we state from the outset that it will be necessary, for the purposes of this chapter, to customize our use of deconstruction somewhat. What we mean by this is that it will be necessary to use the notion less in the terms of a strict critical system applied within the specific philosophical context of the academy, and more in the terms of a generally accessible critique of popular culture more widely. We will need to 'twist' deconstruction a bit when we move out of the strict confines of academic discipline and into the broader realm of psychological culture.

Fourth, it is important to indicate what we mean to include when we speak of 'texts' here. Generally we prefer to use the term in the inclusive sense favoured by Burr (2003) as anything that can be read, as any broad system of signification that can be considered to have, or carry social meaning and discourse. Elsewhere Parker (Parker, 1992; Burman and Parker, 1993; Parker *et al.,* 1995; Parker and the Bolton Discourse Network, 1999) has addressed psy-representations within the specific texts available as cultural resources, e.g. psychology textbooks, clinical case studies, advice columns, films, TV soap operas, talk shows, extracts from newspapers, etc. Here we have preferred not to follow such a strict textual demarcation, both in order to emphasize the breadth of psychological culture, and because this is an open-ended theoretical project rather than an exercise in 'textual empiricism'.

A last key term that we will need to draw on in the ensuing discussion, especially given that we have emphasized the role of subjectivity *in addition* to that of broader forms of social influence, is that of dialectics. We use this term in conjunction with the idea of deconstruction. Dialectics, hopefully, will enable us to think through what psychological culture is doing to psychology and to psychopathology (and not just what psychology and psychopathology are doing to popular culture). In this way, dialectics will serve as a theoretical means of comprehending the ostensibly complementary pairing of deconstruction both 'inside' and 'outside' of psychology. Given that dialectics is not a term that has been, to say the least, enthusiastically adopted by much mainstream psychology, it may prove helpful for us to briefly elaborate on the term. Dialectics is a theoretical framework that enables us to think through relations of contradiction that are, at the same time, complexly interwoven, historically interlaced, and open to change. Dialectical relations exist as a 'unity of opposites' that play themselves out in 'strategies of tension'. Dialectics hence is the gradually resolved synthesis of oppositions, the synthesis, in classical Marxist terms, of thesis and antithesis. Parker has suggested elsewhere (1999b) that the advantage of the dialectical metaphor lies in the fact that it connects the personal and the political. Hence the dialectic, as strategy of tension, is both the condition for us being able to move in one direction or another in our social relationships with one another, and the setting for individual interpersonal activity. Connecting the personal and political in this dialectical way opens up the opportunity to profitably link critical questions of the individual and the social without reducing one to the other. Importantly then, the use of dialectics here will be about comprehending the relations between different forms of critique, and comprehending the relation between the different domains in which the psychological is worked through.

Deconstruction as corroding psychology from within

The first tool we have in contesting the concepts of psychology as they are experienced and represented in psychological culture is, as suggested above, deconstruction. Why is this so? Well, for a start, deconstruction is particularly useful for corroding psychology from within. To explain how this is so, it is useful to sketch something of a 'working sense' of how deconstruction is actually applied. Deconstruction works through a kind of anti-method which resists definition or prescription, and that focuses on how a 'problem' is produced within a text. Just to be clear, the priority in deconstruction is to gain a sense of *how* a 'problem' is produced the way it is rather than wanting to pin it down and say *this* is what it really is (Derrida, 1983; Norris, 1990). A critical focus of deconstruction, then is asking, in a directed and concerted way, how certain aspects of a text are actively *problematized*. What is important about the deconstructive approach here, to crudely paraphrase Derrida (1967/1978), is that 'the stones of the house may be used as the weapons against it'. In other words, with a critical enough engagement with the central texts of psychology, or with the basic premises permeating psychological culture, psychology can be effectively deconstructed even from within on the basis of its own terms of explanation.

There are inherent dangers within such an approach, however, and it is important that we be aware of them. One problem that presents itself to enthusiasts of deconstruction is simply that of taking deconstruction too seriously (as discussed by Norris (1990, 1996)). This would seem something of a paradoxical state of affairs considering what a playful approach deconstruction is. The opposing problem, on the other extreme, is of treating deconstruction as *perpetual play*. This would seem an equally paradoxical state of affairs given that deconstruction is still a serious part of the Enlightenment philosophical tradition, as Derrida (1967/1978) himself insists. Why are these two apparent problems so dangerous? Well, we would venture that they are dangerous – and this is an answer specific to the aims and agendas of critical psychology – because in making them, we lose sight of what has driven critical psychologists to deconstruction in the first place, that is *the peculiarly powerful role that psychology plays in Western culture* (Gordo-López, 2000; De Vos, 2012).

By becoming mired in either an overly playful or an overly serious analysis, we risk losing the distinction between the colonizing force of psychology, on the one hand, and the wider range of social and political actions which it threatens to saturate, on the other. In making such errors, we would be losing sight of the difference between psychological reasoning embedded in psychological culture, and other kinds of moral-political activity. That is, the specific tactical employment of deconstruction inside psychology could all too easily be turned into a fetish which structures one's perceptions of the world. Or, put differently again, by falling prey to these problems, prospective deconstructors risk losing a sense of perspective on the difference between the psychological and the political, and upon how the psychological has attempted, in some ways, to colonize and reformulate what are at basis *political problems, problems of power, social control and regulation.*

At this point it becomes important to complement the notion of a psychological culture with a slightly more forceful conceptualization, that of the *psy-complex*. The psy-complex is a central term to critical psychology. It refers to that intricate network of theories and practices of academic and professional psychology that come to inform our most basic and everyday notions of self, mind, deviance and normality (cf. Ingleby, 1985; Rose, 1990, 1991; Parker, 1997a). Once we are properly able to get a sense of the breadth and power of psychology's influence on Western culture – which the notion of the psy-complex certainly facilitates – then we begin to see the importance of critically applying deconstruction not only from within psychology, but also *from without.*

Deconstruction as corroding psychology from without

We indicated at the outset of this chapter that deconstruction does something different in the realm of popular culture to what it is able to do within the confines of the strictly academic world. For the moment let us say that what deconstruction is able to do outside the academic discipline of psychology, within the realms of contemporary culture, is complementary to the theoretical work of deconstruction *inside* psychology. What deconstruction can do in popular culture it can do inside of psychology as well of course – although it seems *particularly* efficacious to apply this mode of critique to the broader domain of psychological culture – and that is to open up qualities that are attributed to individuals, fixed normative patterns of behaviour, distinct 'psychologies', and to open them up as both 'intentional' and functional. To say that such 'normative patterns of behaviour' or 'discrete psychologies' are functional is to suggest that they maintain a political use, a useful function, as a foothold for power, in the maintenance of certain socio-historically specific power relations. To expand upon this point we might draw on Foucault (1975/1979) to suggest these kinds of ideas of normative psychology are the means through which deviant individuals are problematized as 'abnormal' and in need of the rehabilitative or curative attentions of qualified experts like psychologists. Likewise these 'norms' are the basis upon which individuals may problematize *themselves*; observe, monitor and compare their 'selves' to certain social standards to which they should, at all costs, attempt to conform (Foucault, 1976/1981).

We have seen how deconstruction can be used to corrode psychology from within, to reflect on the methodological working of deconstruction, so now let us turn to the methodological working of this 'method' as way of substantiating how deconstruction may be useful also in corroding psychology from *without.* Not only does deconstruction focus *on how problems are created within texts*, it also focuses on how texts operate to delimit meanings, interpretations and subjectivity (Derrida, 1967/1978; Norris, 1990, 1996; Sarup, 1993). Indeed, a methodological focus in deconstruction is exactly upon how the reader's prospects of understanding and their room for interpretative movement are effectively 'closed down' within texts. One might say that a deconstructive reading is always attentive to how discursive lines of force within texts *position* subjects. A good case in point here is that of the forms of psychotherapy, which, whether of a behaviourist, cognitive or psychoanalytic bent, take for granted certain privileged descriptions of psychopathology, and which may well be shown to oppress people at the same time as they are pretending to help them (cf. Hook, 2001a; Parker 1999a). Deconstruction then directs our attention to exactly *the lack of viable alternative interpretations, positions and understandings within given discourses.* In this way, we might suggest that deconstruction also leads us to explore the ways in which our own problems are *located* in discourse. Similarly, deconstruction leads us to examine how we may make and remake our lives through moral-political projects which are embedded in a sense of justice (Derrida, 1994), rather than merely within given psychiatric discourses. Here we can see then what a reasonable political outcome of a successful deconstruction might be; by the same token, we can see how its effects may be effectively applied on individual (or personal) as well as broader sociopolitical levels of action.

Psychopathology

Having paid some theoretical attention to the possibilities afforded critical psychology by methods of deconstruction, it is now appropriate to attempt to apply these ideas, and to turn more directly to psychopathological practices in the psy-complex. Counselling, psychotherapy and even psychoanalysis sometimes can, in certain circumstances, provide settings for the deconstruction of psychopathology (Parker, 1999b). This is where deconstruction is, in a sense, used as therapy. Instead of being located firmly inside the person as an enduring personality trait, the problem is situated as the product of the historical relationship the person has forged with others. Instead of being something discrete and distinctively abnormal, the problem is positioned in relation to the many varieties of action and experience that structure the 'normal' everyday world (cf. Epston and White, 1989; Fuller and Hook, 2001; Long and Zietkiewicz, 2001). And instead of being solely the property of the person who attends the session as client or patient, the problem is re-specified as being as much to do with the reactions of the designated professional and what goes on between the ordinary person and the expert world (Epston and White, 1989). Theoretical descriptions of family systems and narratives of deficit have each, in various ways, confirmed the idea that psychopathology lies on a continuum with what normal folks do, and that those professionals who pretend to be free from psychopathology are likely to do most damage.

Unfortunately, this is where the baleful influence of psychiatric discourse and practice becomes evident. It is in this context where psychopathology, which operates as a construct which is crucial to the identity and salaries of psychiatrists (and other associated mental health professionals), is imported into therapeutic work, distorting attempts to make sense of problems of living and relating to others. It is particularly useful here to draw on Said's (1983) notion of discourses as languages of control over what they constitute as their special domain. This definition draws attention to how the power constituted by discursive and institutional bases is productive of professional positions; this definition likewise illuminates how a certain discursive/institutional domain delimits the ways in which such problems may be understood. It is in this way that counsellors and psychotherapists might be said to fall victim to the mystification of medical knowledge in psychiatric vocabulary and discourse.

To fall victim to the construction of psychopathology in this manner is to believe that psychiatric expertise rests on a secure collection of brute facts. A certain kind of knowledge is monumentalized in this way, and made largely indisputable. This is dangerous enough to counsellors and psychotherapists, let alone to clients and patients, and there are many possible questionable consequences of this state of affairs. (Hook (2001a, 2001b), for example, demonstrates how psychopathologies are often *discursively* generated within clinical environments, echoing Parker *et al.*'s (1995) earlier contention that diagnostic criteria can often be said to be more *justificatory arguments* than *objective signs.*)

Psychiatric discourse too often succeeds here because it is able to persuade us that it does not itself employ complex theoretical systems to select certain kinds of behaviour and organize them into diagnostic categories. And too many psychiatrists are themselves bewitched by the idea that what they do is grounded in concrete empirical observation free from any theoretical framing. This is also seemingly why so many psychiatrists profess astonishment when they are challenged, why they resort to pathologizing those who disagree with their observations, and why they are a danger to themselves as well as to others.

Psychopathology is a construct, storied into being in numbers of psychiatric texts in books and journals which exceed the numbers of patients diagnosed, and sedimented in practices which make it look and feel substantial and real. But just as it has been constructed, so it can be *deconstructed*. This endeavour is sometimes represented as wholly intuitive or spontaneous, and this is understandable, given the powerful role that expert knowledge plays in many people's lives in contemporary culture. (It is important to bear in mind here Foucault's (1980b) precaution that power can be oppressive and productive at the same time.) It is likewise understandable that when people seize the power to make sense of their lives and relationships they construct that activity as being in some way anti-theoretical. But it is not. When we become experts upon our own lives, as reflexive self-conscious skilled practitioners of the discourse which bears us, as those who are paid to listen or those who pay to speak, we have also become *theoreticians*. An understanding of the construction and deconstruction of psychopathology requires, then, a reflection for a moment on theoretical resources which permit it to exist and permit us to contest it. That is why the book *Deconstructing Psychopathology* was written (Parker *et al.*, 1995).

One theme kept coming up, whether the authorial group was talking about psychopathy or paranoia or psychosis. And this was where some of them tried a very simple deconstructive reversal of the priority that is usually given to psychiatric discourse. What usually happens, of course, is that the psychiatric system and its hangers-on persuade us that psychopaths are out there in the streets, and that we need to rethink community care, for example, and to agree that we need to scoop up the psychopaths and so solve the problem. Or that there are certain people who are paranoid, and somehow we have to get them to see that there are not massive conspiracies that are organizing their lives. Or that mad people speak in a strange schizophrenic word-salad kind of way, and that this psychotic speech can be studied and identified and tied to certain kinds of thought disorders inside people's heads.

You *can* challenge those psychiatric ways of framing social problems by blurring the distinctions that psychiatry makes between the mad and the 'normals'. You can do that by pointing to the ways in which modern society encourages behaviour that is unfeeling and manipulative. You can challenge psychiatric discourse by arguing that it does not make much sense to isolate certain people as psychopathic using those criteria, or by pointing out that many of the conspiracies that people are worried about do turn out to have some basis in fact and so it is dangerous to blame those who are suspicious about the order of things. Similarly, you can point out that word-salads are very widespread in avant-garde literature and plays about schizophrenics, but that it is actually very difficult to find talk like that, and the way people talk when they are supposed to be mad still actually follows normal rules of speech.

All well and good. But some of the authorial group wanted to go a bit further than that, and this is where the arguments started. Some of them wanted to say that if you look at the way that psychiatric discourse, and psychiatrists themselves, operate, it, and they, do seem, in a sense, more psychopathic than those they are treating. This would seem especially the case given that psychiatrists, and arguably the entire psychiatric system, seem pathologically suspicious about ordinary people's behaviour. Likewise, the way psychiatrists talk – that is, the use of psychiatric discourse – appears so removed from everyday experience as to border on the psychotic. The problem is that psychiatrists, and clinical psychologists who wish they were psychiatrists, function as part of institutions and bodies of knowledge that legitimate the psychopathic, paranoid, psychotic things they do to others, and the way *they* speak is treated with such reverence that anyone who questions it is made out to be the crazy one. No, the others in the book would insist, you cannot just say the psychiatrists are the mad ones. Of course, a deconstruction has to be a little more subtle than that. So, they tussled over the question of psychotic discourse, as one example, and arrived at a kind of compromise, which is that the kind of talking and writing that leads to psychiatric diagnosis is 'psychotic'. The fear of psychosis in psychiatric texts and case studies reproduces the fear of madness that structures psychiatry and clinical psychology, and it constitutes that madness as something that is located inside particular people.

Psychotic discourse is not produced by the psychiatrists because they are the mad ones, but it does structure the way the psychiatrists are positioned as the sane speakers who have control over those they place the madness in. Deconstruction does not simply tell us that what we thought was the origin of something is actually only an effect of that something, but it helps us to read texts which keep the origin and the effect apart. We do not, for example, refuse to accept traditional views of thinking because we just want to replace the privileging of individual thought over public dialogue and claim that there is no such thing as individual thought. What we then need to do is to locate those oppositions in systems of power. What a practical deconstruction does is move beyond a reversal of conceptual oppositions that are held in place by power, and locate the problem in the way the discourse operates in institutions.

Dialectics

Dialectics now serves as a theoretical framework to comprehend the ostensibly complementary pairing of deconstruction 'inside' and deconstruction 'outside', as twin corrosive agents inside the apparatus of the psy-complex and outside in psychological culture. It exactly helps us to understand the relation between the two domains and the two forms of critical work as one that is *not* complementary but as dialectical, as interwoven and contradictory, as historically interlaced and as open to change. To open deconstruction to dialectical examination in this way is, of course, to risk totalizing the different domains of critique under one theoretical system; usually when we speak of dialectics the 'system' is that of Marxism. But we would advance the argument that precisely because we are addressing the domain of the psychological here we can also distance ourselves from the temptation either to insert a truly dialectical or Marxist psychology inside the disciplinary apparatus – that is, indeed, what deconstruction necessarily and helpfully forbids – or to romanticize a real human psychology outside in psychological culture – that is what deconstruction in culture necessarily and helpfully prohibits (Parker, 1999c). Dialectics here is not about reinstating something correct in the place of incorrect ideas in either domain but about comprehending the relation between different forms of critique and the relation between different domains in which the psychological is worked through.

Deconstruction of psychopathology, or of anything else, is, in its radical practical form, a *dialectical* unravelling of the way a notion comes to be the way it is such that all that is around it is dependent upon it. This is also, not incidentally, why psychiatry is so desperate to retain the notion. Although some practitioners of deconstruction are queasy about dialectics – usually because they find in their version of deconstruction an easy warrant for liberal pluralism, which they then like to counterpose to the supposed and caricatured certainty and finalism of dialectical critique; and it might move too close to the Marxism they loathe so much – deconstruction rests upon certain dialectical notions. When we grasp these notions we may grasp how we might deconstruct psychopathology, for they help us to comprehend how the discourse and practice of psychiatry confirms its status in the world of counselling and psychotherapy through a series of contradictory, para-doxical conceptual moves. We may summarize these fraudulent and malign moves dialectically by saying that psychopathology is an abstract notion which operates as if it were concrete, and that it is a concrete practice which operates as if it were abstract. This mystifying double operation underpins the power of psychiatric discourse and institutions to make diagnoses and to render other mental health professionals and users susceptible to those diagnostic systems.

Once we uncouple those abstract and concrete aspects of psychopathol-ogy which govern psychiatry as a culturally located, historically specific regime of truth, we will then be in a position to understand the way in which psychopathology fails to work *and* the way in which it does work. A dialec-tical analysis and uncoupling of the abstract and concrete, then, allows us to better engage in abstract and concrete practical deconstruction of psychopa-thology in theory and practice.

Psychopathology operates as if it were abstract by systematically con-cealing the messy, mutually incompatible descriptions of problems which we feel as being inside us and which we try to describe to others. As we grasp descriptions of mental states and what might go wrong with them from already-existing systems of discourse, we confirm to those who listen that they really are descriptions of things outside discourse, inside us. And psychopathology operates as if it were concrete by a mixture of anecdotal accounts, which illustrate how dangerous pathology can be, and case stud-ies, which are presented as the brute reality which is only then theorized.

The abstract, already theoretical, nature of accounts is concealed in each and every story about the supposed realities of pathology.

Now this double mystification in psychopathology as a discursive practice can be grasped dialectically, but it is not sufficient for *us* either to give only a 'theoretical' abstract account or to provide only an 'empirical' concrete rebuttal. What would be missing in either of these one-sided responses would be a fully dialectical engagement with the problem, which addressed at one and the same time the objective *and* the subjective aspects of the problem; that is, how images of normality and pathology function in reality and the subjective grasp they have on us as we read our own experience at each moment as normal or pathological.

It is worth pointing out that Marxism, far from being a closed system, is characterized by praxis and reflexivity. It precisely tries to grasp the nature and interconnection of the objective and subjective. If we take some signal phrases from the theses on Feuerbach (Marx, 1845/1975), for example, we would expect that any Marxism worth the name would home in on 'sensuous human activity', and would be attracted to psychoanalysis as something which might address our location in capitalist culture as an 'ensemble of social relations' (Parker, 1997b).

One of the strengths of deconstruction was that it opened up theory to immanent critique at the very moment that it applied it. But to follow that through we need to connect culture, praxis and reflexivity. Just as Marxism is dialectically woven into the fabric of capitalism, so our present forms of subjectivity are constituted by capitalist culture and by our resistance to that culture. It is constituted in this way as well as being discovered under the surface when we engage in analysis. That discovery comes about through treating subjectivity as a complex contradictory resource rather than as the place where psychopathology lurks, and it can be discovered in the dialectics and deconstruction of life inside and outside psychology.

8 Lacanian social theory and clinical practice

This chapter shifts gear to extend the discussion of deconstruction in psychology to neighbouring areas of work, and to bring into the debate other authors who have become more prominent as sources of critique by those involved in the broad 'social constructionist' movement in the discipline. We have already seen how psychotherapy and counselling has been deeply affected by deconstruction, and in psychoanalysis too there have been repercussions of this way of thinking about language and social relations. In the first uptake of deconstruction in psychology there was often reference to a trio of authors who were, rather misleadingly, gathered together under the rubric of 'post-structuralism': Derrida, Foucault, and the psychoanalyst Jacques Lacan.

As the debates have moved on, other authors, who have each to some degree or another been influenced by Lacan's work, have entered the fray, or rather they have been entered into the arguments against mainstream psychology by critical psychologists who have found their ideas useful to radicalize social constructionist theory. These three additions to our armoury against the discipline are the feminist 'queer' theorist Judith Butler, the 'post-Marxist' discourse theorist Ernesto Laclau, and the Hegelian–Lacanian–Marxist Slavoj Žižek.

In 2000 the three engaged in a sustained debate published in the book *Contingency, Hegemony, Universality*, and my discussion of that debate which was published in a psychoanalytic journal was designed to bring out the main lines of difference between the three writers and to think about what the consequences of their engagement with Lacan's ideas were for clinical practice. The 'clinic' is something that psychologists have always claimed to have something to say about, with 'treatment' following on from research devoted to 'prediction and control'. Our concern with deconstruction should also lead us to have something critical to say about that domain of work.

An intellectual encounter between three writers sympathetic to some degree with Lacan's work has been recorded in the book *Contingency, Hegemony, Universality* (Butler *et al.*, 2000a). These three writers are well known in the overlapping collection of fuzzy sets 'cultural studies', 'literary theory' and 'political theory', and, as the subtitle of the book, *Contemporary Dialogues on the Left*, indicates, they also have some sympathy with Marxist, 'post-Marxist' or feminist politics. One question that the debate between the three often returns to is whether it is possible to articulate Lacanian theory with radical politics. However, another question that is embedded in the encounter but which is only obliquely addressed is whether there are *clinical* implications for the kind of leftist readings of Lacan that these three writers engage in. I focus on that question in this chapter.

Lacan has had a reputation among his English-speaking audience mainly as a 'social theorist', and for some readers only as a source for film criticism, and this has meant that his clinical work as a psychoanalyst has usually been obscured (e.g. Burgin *et al.*, 1986; MacCannell, 1986; Macey, 1988). The actual practice of Lacanian psychoanalysis has been assumed to be of little importance to the way in which the 'social' might be specified and the way political change may be envisaged. The recent attempts to recover Lacan's clinical descriptions and speculations, the primary focus of his work, have then, as a consequence, been trapped into describing a Lacan who speaks about analysis but not much about culture (e.g. Fink, 1997; Nobus, 2000; cf. Leader, 1996, 1997). But perhaps it is now possible to take the realm of 'Lacanian social theory' that has tended to float free of clinical practice, and which is exemplified in this exchange between Butler, Laclau and Žižek, and ground it in that practice again.

Psychoanalysis and subversion

Most attempts to translate psychoanalysis from the realm of the individual, with which clinical practice usually concerns itself, and the social, where the politics of psychoanalysis is addressed, are caught in a dualism between the individual and the social that reproduces each realm as separate and self-sufficient (Henriques *et al.*, 1998). When the social is treated as a collection of individuals to which psychoanalytic theory can most directly and easily be applied, the retranslation back into notions of individual pathology and clinical technique are quite uninteresting, banal even, for the analyst.

The translation back and forth may well entail elements of 'wild analysis' that introduce along the way some new ideas that are fruitful, but not much change in the conceptual relation between the individual and their political world (e.g. Young, 1994). When the social is treated as if it were a gigantic individual, for which developmental sequences and defence mechanisms operate, the translation is not so smooth, and the necessary modifications to psychoanalytic theory may yield, upon retranslation to individual clinical work, insights that tell us something about how the person is culturally located and what the implications might be for psychic and political processes (e.g. Lasch, 1978). Either way, the psychic and the political are still conceived of as interacting, dialectically so perhaps, but as self-contained and antagonistic.

Representation

The debate between Butler, Laclau and Žižek circles around another way to think about this antagonism, and how to relocate the antagonism at the level of *representation*. The deadlock of representation that each of them worries away at opens the way, perhaps, to break from a notion of the individual and social as separate and instead to attend to this deadlock as a constitutive aspect of the social and as constitutive of the individual subject. Antagonism 'between' the individual and the social is then one manifestation of the deadlock of representation rather than its original defining source. Žižek makes the point most explicitly in his argument, against Laclau, that the antagonism is 'internal' to the subject and the social rather than operating 'between' the two.

This project is crucial to any attempt to rethink and rework the entwinement of the 'personal' and the 'political' in socialist politics, an attempt most apparent in socialist feminism in the late 1970s (e.g. Zaretsky, 1976; Rowbotham *et al.*, 1979/2013). Psychoanalysis here, in the guise of Reich and other writers loosely associated with the Frankfurt School tradition, from Object Relations theory and then, to an extent, to Lacan, homed in on the family as site of oppression and on its role as a 'haven in a heartless world', which set up an ambivalence about security and change that spiralled into the heart of individual subjects (e.g. Mitchell, 1974; Lasch, 1978). The key question about the linkage between personal and political change then increasingly becomes the extent to which the experience of that change is 'therapeutic', and the flight into therapy from politics that is such a striking characteristic of the Left since the 1970s becomes the background against which an attempt to politicize individual experience is set and trapped (Jacoby, 1973).

What Butler, Laclau and Žižek do is a little different, precisely because their vantage point on this intersection between the individual and the social is not from the 'personal' side of the equation but from the *political*. The reference points for the debate between the three are rooted in different conceptions of what the historical conditions of possibility and dynamics for change might be: Butler and Žižek are working on the terrain of Hegelian philosophy (against Laclau's post-structuralist reading of Gramsci) but dispute the degree of closure and contradiction that Hegel permits; Žižek and Laclau still take Marxism as a starting point (against Butler's grounding in feminist and post-colonial theory) but disagree over the extent to which ideology and truth necessitate a reading of Marx or a shift to 'post-Marxism'; and Laclau and Butler situate themselves within the framework of new social movements (against Žižek's adherence to a form of Leninism) but accuse each other of retreating to Kantian formalism.

The 'deadlock of representation' also afflicts political dialogue in the book. Those points in the exchange that most directly connect Lacanian psychoanalysis and Marxist political practice, in Žižek's contributions, are also unfortunately the points where the two domains seem to be most incompatible. Laclau complains that while it is possible to debate with Butler, in the case of Žižek 'The only thing one gets from him are injunctions to overthrow capitalism or to abolish liberal democracy, which have no meaning at all' (Laclau, 2000a: 290), 'his discourse is schizophrenically split between a highly sophisticated Lacanian analysis and an insufficiently deconstructed traditional Marxism' (Laclau, 2000b: 205). We finally see a parting of the ways, perhaps, of an alliance between the two writers that goes back to Žižek's favourable reviews of *Hegemony and Socialist Strategy* (Laclau and Mouffe, 1985) and the inclusion of Žižek's (1990) writing in Laclau's later text *New Reflections on the Revolution of Our Time* (1990).

Now Laclau declares that his 'sympathy with Žižek's politics was largely the result of a mirage' (Laclau, 2000a: 292). Žižek's response is merely to insist, after much goading by Laclau to define exactly what political programme he is advocating, that 'opting for the *impossible*' may mean terror and the ruthless exercise of power, and his parting shot in the final chapter in the book is to say that 'if this radical choice is decried by some bleeding heart liberals as *Linksfaschismus*, so be it!' (Žižek, 2000a: 326). This difference over political strategy and the reduction to the political is interesting, but even more telling is Laclau's comment that 'Žižek's thought is not organized around a truly *political* reflection but is, rather, a *psychoanalytic* discourse which draws its examples from the politico-ideological field' (Laclau, 2000a: 286). So, the question is whether there is once again a simple split between psychoanalysis and politics that would explain why Žižek is so objectionable to Laclau, and to a lesser extent to Butler, or whether there is something about genuine psychoanalysis and psychoanalytic practice *in extremis* that would disturb 'bleeding heart liberals', including those favourably disposed to psychotherapy. But to begin to answer that question we would have to know what psychoanalysis is in the discursive terrain mapped out in this debate to start with.

The unconscious and sexuality

One of the striking characteristics of *Contingency, Hegemony, Universality* is that although there are plenty of references to Lacan, when we are invited to take a step back to look at the historical and theoretical antecedents of Lacanian psychoanalysis all three writers lead us to Hegel rather than Freud.

A number of metaphors for the relationship between the individual and what goes beyond them as a condition for being are evoked by Butler, Laclau and Žižek, but there is little direct discussion of the unconscious. Žižek, for example, cites Hegel's description of the plant as an animal with its intestines outside itself in the form of roots, and he then reverses the formula such that we may view the human being as a plant with its roots outside, getting nutrition from the symbolic: 'is not the *symbolic order* a kind of spiritual intestines of the human animal outside its Self' (Žižek, 2000b: 250). This interesting image is not then used to tell us something more about the unconscious, which for Lacanians of course is bound up with the Symbolic order, but it merely serves as another way to bypass Freud altogether.

This Hegelian image of the plant as an animal may look like psychoanalysis and it does trace some aspects of the problematic of personal analysis, and one could make a case that Hegel's 1813 *Logic* includes an insistence on the activity of reflecting on the 'space of reasons' which amounts to something ur-psychoanalytic (Hegel, 1969). But for Lacanians such a line of argument is skewed from the beginning. We start with Freud not Hegel, even though there are clearly Hegelian themes such as the master–slave dialectic and the beautiful soul that are necessarily part of the theoretical apparatus that Lacan brings to his return to Freud.

Butler, Laclau and Žižek sometimes draw upon Freudian concepts (repression, disavowal) as background assumptions, but most often they are happy to ignore them or to replace them with other theoretical elements. Sexuality then tends to be replaced by other quasi-Freudian motifs. For Butler sexual difference is constituted through culturally specific discursive processes and it is upon the two opposed positions that gender and sexuality are performed. The performativity of sex, then, is circumscribed by certain limits, but it is the task of radical social theory and activism – such as the queer movement, which at an early stage dubbed Butler (1990) their patron saint – to disrupt those limits. Each theoretical specification of the parameters within which subjectivity is constituted includes a view of what must be confronted by a subject in analysis, and Butler, Laclau and Žižek mark this as an 'impossibility' which assumes a various and polysemous character. Coming to terms with the impossible stands in the place of the focus on unconscious sexual desire in Freud.

Subversion and political theory

Freud's work was a crucial component of and motor for the Western Enlightenment tradition, and this is precisely one of the ways in which psychoanalysis is most radical. Psychoanalysis is subversive, and recognition of this is one of the unspoken background assumptions in *Contingency, Hegemony, Universality*. This is where Lacan starts to become really important, because what his reading of psychoanalysis does is to bring to the fore the radical unravelling of human experience that Freud opened up. This 'deconstruction' of the subject and of the symbolic determinants of subjectivity is where particular notions of political change start to become useful but where they are also sometimes a liability.

The 'background' for *Contingency, Hegemony, Universality* is Laclau and Mouffe's (1985) *Hegemony and Socialist Strategy* as part of 'an anti-totalitarian, radical democratic project' (Butler *et al.*, 2000b: 1). We might ask whether psychoanalysis is part of this project, to which the three might say yes, but whether individual psychoanalysis is part of this project is another matter altogether.

The key *psychoanalytic*, sometimes latent, issues in the encounter between Butler, Laclau and Žižek are negativity, determination and the particularity of the subject, and we can trace the way these points of focus are blurred and sharpened in relation to the manifest themes of hegemony, contingency and universality. These motifs will allow for an examination of how the Symbolic, the Imaginary and the Real are assumed and tackled by Butler, Laclau and Žižek respectively.

Negativity

The three agree, Butler asserts in the introduction to the debate, 'on the continuing political promise of the Gramscian notion of hegemony' (Butler, 2000a: 13). This notion of hegemony – actually a radical reformulation of Gramsci's – entails a theoretical shift within Marxism from an account of the State under capitalism as 'a body of armed men' that guarantees in the final instance the mystification of the working class by ideology to an account of a 'war of position' between the working class and ruling class in which popular cultural practices are a key site of contestation and the State is included in those practices. One class is 'hegemonic' over the other when it is culturally dominant, and so the task of the Left is to reconfigure the way in which signifiers, such as 'class' or 'nation', function within reactionary or progressive discourse and open up different positions for subjects to occupy. For Laclau, one of the theoreticians of this shift, 'the relatively stable set of all these positions is what constitutes a "hegemonic formation"' (Laclau, 2000c: 71). There is no longer a remainder at the level of the signified – an objective view of exploitation, the historical truth of the class struggle – to be discovered and enjoyed. This Gramscian notion of hegemony came to underpin the political activities of the 'Eurocommunist' parties as they transformed themselves, following the lead of the Italian Communist Party, from parties of the Third International 'Comintern' to broader more inclusive social democratic organizations (cf. Mandel, 1978).

Butler follows Laclau's lead here, and her reading of Hegel is as a theorist of the negativity that insists at the heart of every hegemonic formation. This also means that her account of the place of the individual subject in a hegemonic formation is one that has come to be on the basis of a necessary 'foreclosure': 'every subject emerges on the condition of foreclosure' (Butler, 2000b: 140). She later indexes this statement to a reference to Laplanche (Butler, 2000b: 153) rather than Lacan, and there are some clinical consequences to this view. It would mean that differential diagnosis of clinical structures, in which psychotic structure is indicated by the operation of foreclosure (Lacan, 1981/1993), would now be replaced by an attention to the way every subject is constituted through this operation.

There is also a theoretical displacement here from the level of the subject, and specific choices taken by the subject with respect to foreclosure, repression and disavowal, to the operation of distinct 'discursive practices' that open up subject positions. This displacement is even more marked in the light of Butler's divergence from Laclau with respect to how certain 'signs' or 'signifiers' (and there is an elision of these two terms in the debate between the two) might be fought over in political and personal life: 'I am less certain that the sign ought to be the unit of analysis [as Laclau suggests] . . . the sign must itself be resituated within discursive practices' (Butler, 2000c: 271). It is the attention to the positions made available by conflicting 'discursive practices' that gives rise to an image of fluidity of identities among some of Butler's followers in the realm of 'queer politics', an image that she has tried to dispel (Butler, 1993). The attention to discursive practices does draw attention to ways in which questions posed to the subject as constitutive of their structure (by what right they exist or whether they are a man or a woman, in the case of obsessional or hysteric clinical structure respectively) may be relayed by forms of silence: 'interpellation does not always operate through the name: this silence might be meant for you' (Butler, 2000b: 157). There are implications for how silence in analysis might be conceptualized by the analyst (and analysand), and in itself this would be quite compatible with Lacanian practice.

Feminism and psychoanalysis

What Butler does draw attention to is the importance of feminism as a theoretical resource, and as a conceptual compass point that the analyst may use to make sense of how they are positioned by the analysand. At the very least, women analysands are often drawn to analysis by a puzzling over questions of sexual position and sexuality which they want to understand and which it is not helpful to reduce to the manifestation of hysterical structure (accusation, usually directed at men, and identification, usually with women). And Butler's take on feminism does not search for an underlying 'femininity' which it would be the task of analysis to retrieve, champion and celebrate, as in the writings of Irigaray (1985) for example. That is, rather than fall into the trap of opposing Lacan as a patriarchal analyst in the name of the woman who really does exist, Butler is precisely working with the ways in which identities of any kind are characterized by 'constitutive incompleteness' (Butler, 2000a: 30), which we might easily read as 'lack', but it is lack as culturally and politically located. This location then becomes part of the work of political analysis, and, we might imagine, personal analysis as well.

As well as a refusal of authentic femininity and, instead, an attention to how that femininity is produced as a fantasy (one which governs the activities of many feminists and feminist psychoanalysts), Butler draws on post-colonial writing to show how cultures are defined by what they exclude as other, an other that operates as lure as much as horror. Her attention to the 'constitutive act of cultural translation' (Butler, 2000a: 20) moves from Hegel – 'the individual in his *individual* work already *unconsciously* performs a *universal* work' – to Spivak. What Spivak's (1988) description of the way the speech of the 'subaltern' is always within a dominant hegemonic formation brings to Butler's argument is an attention to the ways forms of racialized identity are constructed within the Symbolic. They do not lie ready formed underneath it to be disclosed by analysis, but will precisely need to be 'de-constructed' by it within speech even as they are spoken.

Part of what might be 'de-constructed', though not necessarily at the level of personal analysis, which would be undertaken within the parameters of a given Symbolic order, is the construction of analytic categories themselves. For example, Butler challenges Žižek over his cultural analysis, which assumes the formal operations that he pretends to detect, and she asks: 'what is the place and time' of this 'performative operation' (of Žižek's example of *Jaws* as *point de capiton* for free-floating inconsistent fears when there is 'the return of the thing to itself' as specified by Hegel). Is it 'restricted to the powers of nominalism within modernity' (Butler, 2000a: 27)? However, she too assumes certain categories as taken for granted. Laclau detects in Butler's argument an equally universalizing motif of 'performance', and he asks, 'is performativity an empty place to be variously filled in different contexts, or is it context-dependent, so that there were societies where there were not performative actions?' (Laclau, 2000b: 189).

The body, fantasy and the Symbolic

For Butler, the body is a key site of social and sexual subversion rather than being a taken-for-granted base and indicator of sexual preference: 'the body must enter into the theorization of norm and fantasy, since it is precisely the site where the desire for the norm takes shape, and the norm cultivates desire and fantasy in the service of its own naturalization' (Butler, 2000b: 155). It also means that Butler is decidedly unhappy with accounts that posit the traumatic encounter with the rule of the signifier as organized by a necessarily Oedipally structured Symbolic order as the originary dividing practice through which masculinity and femininity will be formed. For Butler, 'the very theoretical postulation of the originary trauma presupposes the structuralist theory of kinship and sociality' (Butler, 2000b: 142), and to posit the entry into the Symbolic in this way also presupposes a heteronormative account of sexual identity: 'The formal character of this originary, pre-social sexual difference in its ostensible emptiness is *accomplished* precisely through the reification by which a certain idealized and necessary dimorphism takes hold' (Butler, 2000b: 145). It should be noted here that Butler is closer to Lacan than she thinks. Her critique of Lacan is based on a mistaken view of the Imaginary as a site of fluid identifications in contrast to the Symbolic structured by the Law that holds things in place (Butler, 1993). As Žižek (1999) points out, Butler precisely reverses Lacan's account of the fixity of the Imaginary (revealed, for example, in the certainty of psychotic delusional systems which 'regress' to that order) and the freedom the Symbolic provides as a system of positions.

Even so, Žižek and Laclau both find in her view of the Symbolic an image of free movement that seems a little too optimistic; that is, it is too immediately and directly optimistic in the vein of much US liberal pragmatism. For

Laclau, it is necessary to develop a 'formal analysis of logics' of hegemonic operations that would determine what room for movement in the war of position is possible. Žižek also has a problem with Butler's valorization of the resistance of marginal agents in so far as 'What Butler leaves out of consideration is the way in which *state power itself is split from within and rests on its own obscene spectral underside*' (Žižek, 2000a: 313). Žižek's charge, that Butler fails to recognize the way state power is 'split from within', itself rests upon an identification, which Butler is surely right to refuse, between group identity and the State. Butler's response to the charge is to complain that Žižek 'does not explode this identity into something new' (Butler, 2000c: 276). We might say that the clinical question that this opens is one to do with the predicted speed of change in analysis as the analysand makes a rush towards the door of the consulting room for the last time, a question in which Žižek might be seen to err on the side of hesitation and Butler certainly errs on the side of haste. Butler opens up a view of sexual position that does seem overly flexible, one which is ostensibly at one with the construction of sexual position elaborated by Lacan (1975/1998), but which then, as Laclau points out, smuggles in its own assumptions about the 'performative' nature of human nature.

These baseline assumptions about universal characteristics of human existence haunt the debate between the three, and will reappear in accounts of what must be encountered by the subject at the end of analysis, as we will see when we come to Žižek's deployment of the Real in the analytic act. First, though, let us turn to what Laclau offers to the debate and, perhaps, to clinical work.

Determination

Laclau and Mouffe's (1985) development of Gramsci's account of hegemony in capitalist society is directly counterposed to a traditional Marxist account of ideology, and the theory of hegemony in Laclau's work does already assume some Lacanian coordinates from Althusser's (1971) discussion of psychoanalysis in relation to political analysis. Laclau could be read, then, primarily as a theorist of how the Symbolic is structured so as to produce positions for specific subjects to occupy (in Althusserian terms borrowed from Marx as the 'bearers' or 'supports' of the social structure). However, what Lacan produces in Laclau is not so much an account of society but a theoretically elaborated account of its dissolution. Meaning as failure in Lacan, then, 'effectively translates into the split character of every object of identification – what Laclau calls the ultimate *impossibility of society*' (Stavrakakis, 1999: 39). If Laclau's assertion that there is no such thing as society does seem to uncannily and disturbingly chime with

Margaret Thatcher's view of the matter (Homer, 1996), it also points to another element of Lacan's work that Laclau is preoccupied with, though not often overtly: the Imaginary. There is a question running through Laclau's writing – from the retrieval of the concept of Hegemony with Mouffe (1985) to the debate with Butler and Žižek – concerning the determination of the subject and the relationship between a 'formal analysis of logics' of the social and political identification.

Against Butler's universalizing of 'parodic performances' as spaces of negativity in relation to the Symbolic, Laclau posits his own view of what is universal: 'the social organized as a rhetorical space' (Laclau, 2000c: 78). And the social, when conceptualized as a hegemonic formation, does seem to flow from the activities of individuals moving through it and challenging it, as if Laclau, like Butler, is operating on a view of the Symbolic as a realm which holds things in place which is then reproduced or transformed by activities in another realm of day-to-day local activities. Laclau describes, for example, 'the two different modes ('universalizing' and 'particulariz-ing') which shape a hegemonic, articulating totality' (Laclau, 2000a: 302), and his conception of language is as a space which is fluid enough to main-tain relationships and to allow for them to be challenged: 'The ensemble of the rules, plus those actions which implement/distort/subvert them is what we call "discourse"' (Laclau, 2000a: 284).

One account of the political project elaborated by Laclau and Mouffe carries the subtitle *The Radical Democratic Imaginary* (Smith, 1998), and it may well be because that book captures something of the lure of Imagi-nary space against the Symbolic that Laclau detests it, citing it as 'a crude example' which 'confuses analysis of the concrete with purely factual and journalistic accounts' (Laclau, 2000c: 87). It would seem that to be 'soci-ologistic' and 'descriptive' are, for Laclau, as bad as the 'empiricism' that he detects in Butler's work. This is not to say that Laclau is simply stuck in the line of the Imaginary, but that his work is preoccupied with the way in which forms of identification can be avoided through theoretical elabora-tion. What might the analytic implications of this be?

Identification and identity

Laclau looks to 'a horizon of intelligibility of the social which is governed not in *topographies* but in *logics*' (Laclau, 2000c: 58), and he indexes this opposition to one between the State and civil society. One might conceive of the space of psychoanalytic practice as lying precisely in this space. And (somewhat paradoxically, given the concern with identification in Laclau's writings), this would allow for a distinction between, on the one hand, the speech of the subject as concerned with 'topographies' and affairs of the 'state' which we might interpret as lying on the line of the Imaginary – manifest perhaps in attempts to make directly observable political identifications and alliances the matter of analytic dialogue – and, on the other, the 'logics' which may serve to map out the positions in 'civil society' that the subject occupies as positions governed by the Symbolic.

The forms of 'social bond' specified by Lacan (1991/2007) in his discussion of the four discourses, for example, simultaneously locate the subject within social structures (of bureaucracy and education) and in the analytic session (of hysteria and analysis). This specification of the social bond is also one of the points at which Lacan is elaborating 'mathemes' which will precisely map the position of the subject in terms of 'logics'. Laclau's proposal at the level of the social, then, could be quite compatible with the way the analyst may shift from 'understanding' the analysand (the 'meaning' of their speech within an Imaginary relation) to 'formalizing' the symptom and the direction of the treatment (the structure of their speech within the Symbolic).

Laclau takes a position against any form of 'identity politics', and without even the strategic considerations that would be given to this form of politics by Butler. This does not at all mean that he dispenses with identity as a political analytical tool. In fact, part of the shift from class analysis in traditional Marxism to 'post-Marxist' analysis of discourse and hegemonic formations is precisely underpinned by a reduction of class-consciousness to identity. So, in opposition to Žižek, Laclau rehearses his oft-told argument that 'class struggle is just one species of identity politics, and one which is becoming less and less important in the world in which we live' (Laclau, 2000b: 203). Again, we can see an opposition being set up between a conception of society that is held by traditional politics obsessed with the 'relations of production' (including Marxism) and another sphere of action in which political identities are formed; 'class antagonism . . . takes place between those relations [of production] and the identity of the workers outside them' (Laclau, 2000b: 202). And again it is possible to detect in this opposition an opposition between the structurally determined Symbolic order and a more fluid Imaginary realm. Laclau does not want to wish away this realm of political identities in favour of action at the level of the Symbolic; rather, he advertises a variety of new political identities which can be mobilized alongside (and instead of) class: 'The notion of "combined and uneven development" had already pointed out the emergence of complex, non-orthodox political identities and the agencies of revolutionary change' (Laclau, 2000b: 203).

One might imagine an analytic strategy, then, that would home in on the unravelling of forms of political identity that are used by the analysand as a form of defence. The mistake as far as Laclau is concerned, and for a Lacanian psychoanalyst as well here, would be to assume an underlying identity that needs to be retrieved or shored up. Analysis does not abolish the Imaginary identifications that comprise 'identity' but reconfigures it so that the subject recognizes the way those identifications operate. Matters would be a little different in the case of an analysand with psychotic structure, for whom the shoring up of the delusional system would be the preferred option in therapeutic work as opposed to analytic work. Laclau, like Butler, describes the social as comprising subjects who are neurotic rather than psychotic and as not differentiated any further into obsessional or hysteric clinical structures. It is, Laclau argues, the formal distinction between signifier and signified that 'allows the exploration of the unconscious to detach itself from the search for ultimate meaning' (Laclau, 2000c: 69).

Personal analysis as a political lesson

In this vision, then, there is an almost perfect symmetry between personal analysis and the production of a subject who would be functional in a democratic society. In fact, for Laclau, the abandonment of the search for ultimate meaning is as much a watchword for democratic politics as it is for psychoanalysis: 'The only democratic society is one which permanently shows the contingency of its own foundations – in our terms, permanently keeps open the gap between the ethical moment and the normative order' (Laclau, 2000c: 86). There is always already built into Laclau's analysis, then, an account of lack, and an attempt to arrive at the fullness of liberation at the end of analysis would be seen to be as futile as the attempt to arrive at the fullness of liberation at the end of a revolution: 'The elimination of all representation is the illusion accompanying the notion of a *total* emancipation' (Laclau, 2000c: 57), and it would mean 'the end of all hegemonic relation . . . and . . . of all democratic politics' (Laclau, 2000c: 57). On this point, Butler is with Laclau, and she states her position in terms very close to his: 'Paradoxically . . . democracy is secured precisely through its resistance to realization' (Butler, 2000c: 268).

While Laclau does theorize the social in terms of 'logics' he cautions against the adoption of a metanarrative, and in this, of course, he is very much at one with the 'post-Marxist' and 'postmodern' turn to diverse language games in the place of an understanding of historical process. It could be argued that it is not possible to conceptualize what goes on in the historical process and our place in it without a theoretical metanarrative of some kind, and that it is not possible to conceptualize what goes on in the hysterical process of questioning in psychoanalysis and our place in it unless we employ some theoretical metanarrative. The recognition that there is no 'metalanguage', no 'Other of the Other', no 'sexual relation' is very different from a refusal of the theoretical apparatus that we make use of to direct the treatment such that the analysand comes to discover those things for themself. As Žižek points out, 'one needs a kind of metanarrative that explains this very passage from essentialism to the awareness of contingency' (Žižek, 2000c: 106).

Žižek also objects to the political presuppositions that appear in Laclau's own account, and what they obscure, and it is exactly the reduction of class struggle to class 'identity' that he deplores: 'in this silent suspension of class analysis . . . we are dealing with an exemplary case of the mechanism of ideological *displacement*' (Žižek, 2000c: 97). What Žižek's objection does, at the very least, draw attention to, is the way the direction of the treatment in Laclau's vision would too perfectly mirror his political vision: postmodern politics 'does *not* in fact repoliticize capitalism, because *the very notion and form of the "political" within which it operates is grounded in the "depoliticization" of the economy*' (Žižek, 2000c: 98). Perhaps the problem here is not so much the direction of the treatment in analysis as such, for here Laclau's work would translate into an analytic practice perfectly compatible with Lacanian psychoanalysis, but the mirroring that is assumed between the realm of personal analysis and the realm of political action.

This mirroring, then, closes the gap between the two realms, and thus closes the very gap that makes personal change and political action possible. Laclau's work does not explicitly take into account the disparity or space between what the analysand may discover about representation and what political action may be opened up to deal with structural social inequalities. An analytic act may correspond to a social act, but it may be the *difference* between the two that makes each of them possible. To develop some kind of metanarrative would allow us to grasp that we need to turn to an account of the Real and the particularity of the subject.

Particularity of the subject

Žižek accuses Butler and Laclau of being 'secret Kantians'; that is, 'they both propose an abstract a priori formal model (of hegemony, of gender performativity . . .)' and this leads to an 'endless process of complex partial displacements' (Žižek, 2000c: 111). The very account of hegemonic formations that Laclau employs to develop a 'logic', then, traps him in a certain limited horizon, an abstract account of 'radical democracy' that is necessarily blind to the class struggle that could blow apart the hegemonic formation that pertains to capitalist society. Žižek writes as a tactician who has operated as the mouthpiece of a variety of hegemonic formations, from time as speechwriter to the Stalinists when they were in power in Slovenia to activity in the leadership of the Liberal Democratic Party in opposition and then as governors of new free-market Slovenia administering 'shock therapy' to the economy (Boynton, 1998). The guise he adopts in the debate with Butler and Laclau is now as the only one willing to open up the terms of the debate beyond the abstract formal limits of capitalist society, and to bring to bear a different form of 'historicity' that will link Lacan with Marx. So, as opposed to 'historicism', which looks at the play of substitutions within the same fundamental field of substitution, which is what Žižek claims Butler and Laclau do, '*historicity* proper makes thematic different structural principles of this very (im)possibility' (Žižek, 2000c: 112).

Žižek takes as his model of the 'structural principles' of '(im)possibility' the dictum that 'there's no such thing as a sexual relationship' (Lacan, 1975/1998: 12). As Žižek points out, for Lacan, 'every translation of sexual difference into a set of symbolic opposition(s) is doomed to fail, and it is this very "impossibility" that opens up the terrain of the hegemonic struggle for what "sexual difference" will mean' (Žižek, 2000c: 111); this is why sexual difference '*resists* every attempt at its symbolization' (Žižek, 2000c: 111). So far, this account differs from Butler in the sense that it posits sexual difference as a 'dimorphism' that is founded upon a traumatic encounter (which, as we have seen, she disputes as in itself restrictive of the possibilities of a radical subversion and transformation in sexual position and sexuality), and it differs from Laclau in so far as it restricts the dimension of real impossibility to sexual division.

The traumatic kernel of the real

Rather than restrict this 'impossibility' to sex alone, Žižek indexes it to the classic study by Lévi-Strauss (1963) of the Winnebago tribe in Canada. If one group in the tribe was asked to provide a representation of the tribe they drew a circle with another circle inside it (indicating the position of one group surrounded by the other), but if the other group was asked to provide a representation they drew a circle with a line down the centre (indicating the two groups side by side). This perfectly captures the way in which disagreement between the two groups is also a disagreement over what the terms of the disagreement are, and it also nicely illuminates the stakes of disagreement between men and women. Lacan's (1975/1998) diagram of sexuation elaborates just such a mismatch of representations of what the difference is. This is a difference which is, as Žižek points out, a constitutive impossibility of representation, and Lévi-Strauss shows a 'hidden reference to this constant "traumatic kernel" . . . a fundamental antagonism' (Žižek, 2000c: 112).

This traumatic kernel of the real is referred to by Lévi-Strauss as a 'zero-institution', and Žižek extrapolates this to talk of the 'zero-institution' of the 'nation' and 'sexual difference' (Žižek, 2000c: 114). Žižek refers to Hardt and Negri's (2000) account of contemporary capitalism as the closest to a 'model of an analysis' (Žižek, 2000b: 239), and it is capitalism that he takes as the fundamental matrix of the subject's traumatic encounter with the real that they must encounter again, presumably, in personal analysis. However, we should note his enthusiastic citation of the assertion that 'one's own privileged experiences are bad and reactionary arguments' (Deleuze, 1995: 11, cited by Žižek, 2000a: 328, n. 9). For Žižek, 'a personal life-narrative, say, is a *bricolage* of ultimately failed attempts to come to terms with some trauma' (Žižek, 2000c: 125), and the trauma he signals as a key point of impossibility which is sutured over in Laclau's (and Butler's) writing is that of *class*. This raises a number of questions for how psychoanalysis might proceed if it shifted attention from sexual difference to class difference as a 'traumatic kernel' of the Real that must be encountered by the subject.

We would need to have some idea as to whether we should interpret the displacement from class (as Žižek would seem to see it in standard psycho-analytic treatment) because it is a displacement as a defence mechanism. It is characterized by him as an ideological mechanism, so could we then read 'ideological displacement' as operative in each individual subject in analysis under capitalism? Would the non-relation between analyst and analysand then be understood as indicative of a deadlock of representation that was determined by class difference rather than sexual difference? And would this then require a different kind of 'diagram of class struggle' that would reconfigure Lacan's diagram of sexuation?

It would also seem axiomatic here that if we reflexively situate ourselves in the relation with the analysand as a non-relation, the way the deadlock is formalized by the analyst would be itself different from the way it would be formulated from the position of the analysand. What the diagram of sexu-ation indicates is that the very ground rules of disagreement over how the diagram might be interpreted would be interpreted differently from each side. We might say that this necessary difficulty of interpretation respects 'absolute difference' as an end of analysis between analyst and analysand as well as 'absolute difference' in the conception the analysand has of the play of signifiers (cf. Lacan, 1964/1973: 276). What Žižek's account draws attention to, then, is the very way in which a different account may be given of the end of analysis by the analyst and the analysand – a phenomenon already taken seriously by Lacanians in discussions of the 'pass' through which an account is given to the analytic school of the end of analysis (Dunand, 1995).

Žižek (1999) has elsewhere indicated his unease with the late Lacanian argument that a coming to terms with sexuation should be an encounter with the Real that characterizes the end of analysis. For Žižek, this reduction to the difference between men and women operates within a limited historical point of relations between the sexes. His own specification of 'class struggle' as a key point could be defended as appropriate to capitalism, as a fully historicized 'traumatic kernel', but it would still orient the analyst, and the analysand through the direction of the treatment, to a particular kind of end of analysis, and a particular kind of analytic act.

The analytic act

Žižek describes 'the act' as we would expect it to occur in analysis as 'a gesture which, by definition, touches the dimension of some impossible Real' (Žižek, 2000c: 121). But the way he elaborates this act in relation to an act which disturbs the social because it touches the Real of a fundamental structuring antagonism opens up a number of questions for how individual analysis connects with social analysis at the level of changing the world rather than simply interpreting it. 'An authentic act', Žižek argues, 'disturbs the underlying fantasy, attacking it from the point of "social symptom"' (Žižek, 2000c: 124), and here Žižek is referring to the traversing of the fundamental fantasy which has held the subject in place, but in such a way that will embed what an act will be for the subject in their location in the social. That is, the end of analysis in which the analysand goes through the fantasy that has fascinated and immobilized them would be seen as strictly equivalent to the kind of intervention a political activist might make in a hegemonic formation which structures the fantasy lives of those subject to it.

This would also mean that, with respect to the direction of the treatment, the analyst would be drawn into at the very least a theoretical account of how it is that the analysand as a proletarian political actor (say) in relation to class antagonism, rather than as simply a male or female subject in relation to sexuation, comes to engage in an act that was 'authentic' or 'inauthentic'. Žižek draws his own distinction between the act of a leftist (which engages with the Real of an antagonism running through the social) and the act of a fascist (which requires the falsity of locating the antagonism, in corporatist fashion, outside the social, rather than accepting the real antagonism inside it).

Laclau objects to Žižek on three counts: that he sees class as necessarily universalized, that he adheres to a base/superstructure model, and that he makes a strict distinction between struggles that are against the system and those that are intra-systemic. In addition, Laclau points out that capitalism cannot be the Real, as Žižek argues, because it operates as part of the Symbolic. The Lacanian Real is that which resists symbolization. Butler, for her part, objects to what she detects as a Kantian motif in Žižek's insistence that the structures that he describes are prior to the account that he gives of them: 'we cannot identify such [formal] structures first and then apply them to their examples, for in the instance of their "application" they become something other than what they were' (Butler, 2000a: 26). The accusation that Žižek throws against Butler and Laclau thus returns to haunt him, and his insistence on class struggle as the fundamental antagonism which must be tackled in any form of analysis is reduced to the fetish around which his own 'metanarrative' revolves.

What is Left?

It is as difficult to pinpoint and assess the political positions advocated by these three social theorists as it is to discover clinical consequences of their various arguments (Roberts, 2001). Butler has appeal to a new feminist audience that is also suspicious of essentializing femininity, and Laclau has a similar appeal to a 'post-Marxist' constituency wary of brute truth about the economy and history. In both, however, it is exactly their refusal of fixed political positions that prevents them from elaborating a programme for change, though they will engage with already-existing local initiatives. Even Žižek, who outflanks the other two from the Left with the ostensibly most orthodox Marxist rhetoric, is very slippery when it comes to specifying where he stands in relation to Marxist politics (Homer, 2001).

Perhaps it is this very indeterminacy of political programme that makes each of these writers compatible with Lacanian psychoanalysis. We do not try to 'understand' what an analysand is telling us, and we do not 'interpret' to them what the meaning is of what they say. Still less do we educate them to view the world as we do, and 'absolute difference' must include difference over political perspective even when recognition of difference in political perspective comes to serve as an orientation for how one might approach politics.

The very difference of political perspective between Butler, Laclau and Žižek would seem to indicate that psychoanalytic practice with individuals could not be read off easily from the deadlock of representation. In fact the 'impossibility' of representation appears to lie as much in the particular specifications for political action as it does in the way 'impossibility' should be conceptualized. The three do seem to exist in some deadlock that is unsurpassable. It would not, in any case, be appropriate to detect the real underlying political position of Butler, Laclau and Žižek and then to speculate about how this position would play its way out in analysis. The real underlying political position is as much something to be given up as it is something to be refound. One could say that a lesson entirely compatible with Lacanian analysis that these three writers offer is that a 'political position' holds the subject in place while it seems to offer the subject the way out.

With respect to the end of the analysis and the function of the object a (the Lacanian name for the lost object cause of desire), 'by cutting himself loose from the precious object through whose possession the enemy kept him in check, the subject gives the space of free action' (Žižek, 2000c: 122). As if only at that point that we are able to give up what has held us in thrall will we be able to do something different with our lives, and then we will perhaps be different too. It is in that respect that Butler, Laclau and Žižek link the personal and the political and provoke some thinking through of social theory in the realms of clinical practice.

References

Alajoki, A. (2003) *Home from Home*, BBC Video Nation, 24 March, http://www.bbc.co.uk/manchester/videonation/2003/05/home_from_home.shtml (accessed 17 February 2014).

Allen, L. (1993) 'The politics of therapy: An interview with Michael White', *Human Systems: The Journal of Systemic Consultation and Management*, 4, 19–32.

Althusser, L. (1971) *Lenin and Philosophy, and Other Essays*. London: New Left Books.

Antaki, C. and Widdicombe, S. (eds) (1998) *Identities in Talk*. London: Sage

Armistead, N. (ed.) (1974) *Reconstructing Social Psychology*. Harmondsworth: Penguin.

Ayer, A.J. (ed.) (1968) *The Humanist Outlook*. London: Pemberton.

Banister, P., Burman, E., Parker, I., Taylor, M. and Tindall, C. (1994) *Qualitative Methods in Psychology: A Research Guide*. Milton Keynes: Open University Press.

Barthes, R. (1957/1973) *Mythologies*. London: Paladin.

Barthes, R. (1977) *Image – Music – Text*. London: Fontana.

Bateson, G. (1972) *Steps to an Ecology of Mind*. New York: Ballantine.

Bentall, R. (1992) 'Reconstructing psychopathology', *The Psychologist: Bulletin of the British Psychological Society*, 5(2), 61–65.

Bhaskar, R. (1989) *Reclaiming Reality: A Critical Introduction to Contemporary Philosophy*. London: Verso.

Bhavnani, K.-K. (1990) 'What's power got to do with it? Empowerment and social research', in, I., Parker and J. Shotter, (eds) *Deconstructing Social Psychology*. London: Routledge.

Bilefsky, D. (2006) 'Monster band has Finland fretting over face it shows', *New York Times*, 17 April, http://www.nytimes.com/2006/04/17/world/europe/17iht-finn.html (accessed 18 February 2014).

Billig, M. (1985) 'Prejudice, categorization and particularization: From a perceptual to a rhetorical approach', *European Journal of Social Psychology*, 15, 79–103.

Blackman, L. (1994) 'What is doing history? The use of history to understand the constitution of contemporary psychological objects', *Theory & Psychology*, 4(4), 485–504.

Booth, R. and Smith, H. (2006) 'Oh Lordi: From the land of Sibelius, a song for Satan', *The Guardian*, 22 May, p. 3.

Boynton, R.S. (1998) 'Enjoy your Žižek!: An excitable Slovenian philosopher examines the obscene practices of everyday life – including his own', *Linguafranca: The Review of Academic Life*, 7(7), http://linguafranca.mirror.theinfo.org/9810/zizek.html (accessed 19 February 2014).

Bugental, J. and Thomas, J. (1967) *Challenges of Humanistic Psychology*. New York: McGraw Hill.

Burgin, V., Donald, J. and Kaplan, C. (eds) (1986) *Formations of Fantasy*. London: Methuen.

Burman, E. (ed.) (1998) *Deconstructing Feminist Psychology*. London: Sage.

Burman, E. (2006) 'Emotions and reflexivity in feminised education action research', *Educational Action Research*, 14(3), 315–332.

Burman, E. (2007) 'Between orientalism and normalisation: Cross-cultural lessons from Japan for a critical history of psychology', *History of Psychology*, 16(2), 179–198.

Burman, E. (2008) *Deconstructing Developmental Psychology* (second edition). Abingdon/New York: Routledge.

Burman, E., Aitken, G., Alldred, P., Allwood, R., Billington, T., Goldberg, B., Gordo-López, A.J., Heenan, C., Marks, D. and Warner, S. (1996a) *Psychology Discourse Practice: From Regulation to Resistance*. London: Taylor & Francis.

Burman, E., Alldred, P., Bewley, C., Goldberg, B., Heenan, C., Marks, D., Marshall, J., Taylor, K., Ullah, R. and Warner, S. (1996b) *Challenging Women: Psychology's Exclusions, Feminist Possibilities*. Buckingham: Open University Press.

Burman, E. and Parker, I. (eds) (1993) *Discourse Analytic Research: Repertoires and Readings of Texts in Action*. London/New York: Routledge.

Burr, V. (2003) *Social Constructionism* (second edition). London/New York: Routledge.

Butchart, A. (1997) 'Objects without origins: Foucault in South Africa', *South African Journal of Psychology*, 27(2), 101–110.

Butler, J. (1990) *Gender Trouble: Feminism and the Subversion of Identity*. London: Routledge.

Butler, J. (1993) *Bodies That Matter*. London: Routledge.

Butler, J. (2000a) 'Restaging the universal: Hegemony and the limits of formalism', in J. Butler, E. Laclau and S. Žižek, *Contingency, Hegemony, Universality: Contemporary Dialogues on the Left*. London: Verso.

Butler, J. (2000b) 'Competing universalities', in J. Butler, E. Laclau and S. Žižek, *Contingency, Hegemony, Universality: Contemporary Dialogues on the Left*. London: Verso.

Butler, J. (2000c) 'Dynamic conclusions', in J. Butler, E. Laclau and S. Žižek, *Contingency, Hegemony, Universality: Contemporary Dialogues on the Left*. London: Verso.

Butler, J., Laclau, E. and Žižek, S. (2000a) *Contingency, Hegemony, Universality: Contemporary Dialogues on the Left*. London: Verso.

Butler, J., Laclau, E. and Žižek, S. (2000b) 'Introduction', in J. Butler, E. Laclau and

S. Žižek, *Contingency, Hegemony, Universality: Contemporary Dialogues on the Left*. London: Verso.

Cecchin, G. (1992) 'Constructing therapeutic possibilities', in S. McNamee and K.J. Gergen (eds) *Therapy as Social Construction*. London: Sage.

Cecchin, G., Lane, G. and Ray, W.A. (1993) 'From strategizing to non-intervention: Toward irreverence in systemic practice', *Journal of Marital and Family Therapy*, 19, 125–136.

Chang, J. and Phillips, M. (1993) 'Michael White and Steve de Shazer: new directions in family therapy', in S. Gilligan and R. Price (eds) *Therapeutic Conversations*. New York: Norton.

Chasin, R. and Herzig, M. (1994) 'Creating systemic interventions for the sociopolitical arena', in B.B. Gould and D.H. DeMuth (eds) *The Global Family Therapist: Integrating the Personal, Professional, and Political*. New York: Allyn and Bacon.

Cohen, C.I. (1986) 'Marxism and psychotherapy', *Science and Society*, 1(1), 4–24.

Cohen de Lara-Kroon, N. (n.d.) 'Historical overview of projective testing', http://www.cohendelara.com/pdf/chapter_02.pdf (accessed 19 February 2014).

Coleman, R. (1997) *From Victim to Victor: Hearing Voices*. Runcorn: Handsell.

Coleman, R. (1998) *The Politics of the Madhouse*. Runcorn: Handsell.

Coltart, N.E.C. (1988) 'The assessment of psychological-mindedness in the diagnostic interview', *British Journal of Psychiatry*, 153, 819–820.

Crellin, C. (1992) 'Whatever happened to plant psychology?', *History and Philosophy of Psychology Newsletter*, 15, 25–32.

Davies, B. and Harré, R. (1990) '"Positioning": The discursive production of selves', *Journal for the Theory of Social Behaviour*, 20(1), 43–63.

de Shazer, S. (1985) *Keys to Solution in Brief Therapy*. New York: Norton.

de Shazer, S. (1991) *Putting Difference to Work*. New York: Norton.

De Vos, J. (2012) *Psychologisation in Times of Globalisation*. Abingdon/New York: Routledge.

Deleuze, G. (1995) *Negotiations*. New York: Columbia University Press.

Derrida, J. (1967/1978) *Writing and Difference*. London: Routledge & Kegan Paul.

Derrida, J. (1980) 'An interview', *The Literary Review*, 14, 21–22.

Derrida, J. (1981) *Positions*. London: Athlone Press.

Derrida, J. (1983) 'Letter to a Japanese friend', in D. Wood and R. Bernasconi (eds) *Derrida and Différance*. Evanston, IL: Northwestern University Press.

Derrida, J. (1994) 'Spectres of Marx', *New Left Review*, 205, 31–58.

Doherty, J., Graham, E. and Malek, M. (eds) (1992) *Postmodernism and the Social Sciences*. London: Macmillan.

Dreier, O. (1997) *Subjectivity and Social Practice*. Aarhus: Skriftserie.

Dunand, A. (1995) 'The end of analysis (II)', in R. Feldstein, B. Fink and M. Jaanus (eds) *Reading Seminar XI: Lacan's Four Fundamental Concepts of Psychoanalysis*. New York: SUNY Press.

Eagleton, T. (1983) *Literary Theory: An Introduction*. Oxford: Blackwell.

Edwards, D. and Potter, J. (1992) *Discursive Psychology*. London: Sage.

Epston, D. (1993) 'Internalizing discourses versus externalizing discourses', in S. Gilligan and R. Price (eds) *Therapeutic Conversations*. New York: Norton.

References 111

Epston, D. and White, M. (1989) *Literate Means to Therapeutic Ends*. Adelaide: Dulwich Centre Publishing.

Evans, D. (1996) *An Introductory Dictionary of Lacanian Psychoanalysis*. London: Routledge.

Evans, E.P. (1906/1987) *The Criminal Prosecution and Capital Punishment of Animals: The Lost History of Europe's Animal Trials*. London: Faber & Faber.

Fernando, S. (1988) *Race and Culture in Psychiatry*. London: Tavistock.

Fink, B. (1997) *A Clinical Introduction to Lacanian Psychoanalysis: Theory and Technique*. Cambridge, MA: Harvard University Press.

Foucault, M. (1961/2009) *History of Madness*. Abingdon/New York: Routledge.

Foucault, M. (1975/1979) *Discipline and Punish: The Birth of the Prison*. Harmondsworth: Penguin.

Foucault, M. (1976/1981) *The History of Sexuality Volume I: An Introduction*. Harmondsworth: Penguin.

Foucault, M. (1977) *Language, Counter-Memory, Practice: Selected Essays and Interviews*. Oxford: Blackwell.

Foucault, M. (1980a) 'Truth is in the future', in S. Lotringer, (ed.) *Foucault Live: Collected Interviews, 1961–1984*. New York: Semiotext(e).

Foucault, M. (1980b) *Power/Knowledge: Selected Interviews and Other Writings 1972–1977*. Brighton: Harvester Press.

Fuller, S. and Hook, D. (2001) 'Rewriting the body, re-authoring the expert, reading the anorexic body', in D. Hook and G. Eagle (eds.) *Psychopathology and Social Prejudice*. Cape Town: University of Cape Town Press.

Gamaliel (2002) 'The naked time', *E2 Star Trek Episode Guide*, http://everything2.com/title/The+Naked+Time (accessed 19 February 2014).

Garfinkel, H. (1967) *Studies in Ethnomethodology*. New York: PrenticeHall.

Gergen, K.J. (1985) 'The social constructionist movement in modern psychology', *American Psychologist*, 40, 266–275.

Gordo-López, A.J. (2000) 'On the psychologization of critical psychology', *Annual Review of Critical Psychology*, 2, 55–71.

Greening, T. (1998) 'Five postulates of humanistic psychology', *Journal of Humanistic Psychology*, 38(1), 9.

Grieves, L. (1997) 'From beginning to start: The Vancouver Anti-Anorexia League', *Gecko*, 2, 78–88.

Griffith, J. and Griffith, M. (1992) 'Owning one's epistemological stance in therapy', *Dulwich Centre Newsletter*, 1, 5–11.

Gronemeyer, M. (1992) 'Helping', in W. Sachs (ed.) *The Development Dictionary: A Guide to Knowledge as Power*. London: Zed Books.

Hardt, M. and Negri, A. (2000) *Empire*. Cambridge, MA: Harvard University Press.

Hare-Mustin, R.T. and Marecek, J. (1997) 'Abnormal and clinical psychology: The politics of madness', in D. Fox and I. Prilleltensky (eds) *Critical Psychology: An Introduction*. London: Sage.

Harré, R. (1979) *Social Being: A Theory for Social Psychology*. Oxford: Blackwell.

Harré, R. (1981) 'The positivist-empiricist approach and its alternative', in P. Reason and J. Rowan (eds) *Human Inquiry: A Sourcebook of New Paradigm Research*. Chichester: Wiley.

Harré, R. (1983) *Personal Being: A Theory for Individual Psychology*. Oxford: Basil Blackwell.

Harré, R. (ed.) (1986) *The Social Construction of Emotion*. Oxford: Blackwell.

Harré, R. and Secord, P.F. (1972) *The Explanation of Social Behaviour*. Oxford: Blackwell.

Heelas, P. and Lock, A. (eds) (1981) *Indigenous Psychologies: The Anthropology of the Self*. London: Academic Press.

Hegel, G.W.F. (1969) *Science of Logic*. Oxford: Oxford University Press.

Henriques, J., Hollway, W., Urwin, C., Venn, C. and Walkerdine, V. (1998) *Changing the Subject: Psychology, Social Regulation and Subjectivity*. London: Routledge.

Henwood, K. and Parker, I. (eds) (1994) *Qualitative Social Psychology* (Special Issue), *Journal of Community and Applied Social Psychology*, 4 (4).

Homer, S. (1996) 'Psychoanalysis, representation, politics: On the (im)possibility of a psychoanalytic theory of ideology?', *The Letter: Lacanian Perspectives on Psychoanalysis*, 7, 97–109.

Homer, S. (2001) 'It's the political economy stupid! On Žižek's Marxism', *Radical Philosophy*, 108, 7–16.

Hook, D. (2001a) 'Therapeutic discourse, co-construction, interpellation, role-induction: Psychotherapy as iatrogenic treatment modality?', *The International Journal of Psychotherapy*, 6(1), 47–66.

Hook, D. (2001b) 'Psychotherapy, discourse and the production of psychopathology', in D. Hook and G. Eagle (eds) *Psychopathology and Social Prejudice*. Cape Town: University of Cape Town Press.

House, R. and Totton, N. (eds) (1997) *Implausible Professions: Arguments for Pluralism and Autonomy in Psychotherapy and Counselling*. Ross-on-Wye: PCCS Books.

Illich, I. (1976) *Limits to Medicine: The Expropriation of Health*. Harmondsworth: Penguin.

Immelman, A. (1999) 'Inside the mind of Milosevic', Unit for the Study of Personality in Politics, St John's University, Collegeville, MN, http://www1.csbsju.edu/uspp/Milosevic/Milosevic.html (accessed 19 February 2014).

Immelman, A. (2003) 'Psychological profile of Saddam Hussein', Unit for the Study of Personality in Politics, St John's University, Collegeville, MN, http://www1.csbsju.edu/uspp/Research/Saddam%20profile.html (accessed 19 February 2014).

Ingleby, D. (1985) 'Professionals as socializers: The "psy complex"', *Research in Law, Deviance and Social Control*, 7, 79–109 (reprinted in I. Parker (ed.) (2011) *Critical Psychology: Critical Concepts in Psychology, Volume 1, Dominant Models of Psychology and Their Limits*. London/New York: Routledge).

Irigaray, L. (1985) *The Sex Which Is Not One*. Ithaca, NY: Cornell University Press.

Jacoby, R. (1973) 'The politics of subjectivity: Slogans of the American New Left', *New Left Review*, 79, 37–49.

Jacoby, R. (1975) *Social Amnesia: A Critique of Conformist Psychology from Adler to Laing*. Hassocks: Harvester Press.

Kitzinger, C. and Perkins, R. (1993) *Changing Our Minds: Lesbian Feminism and Psychology*. New York: New York University Press.

Knight, M. (ed.) (1961) *Humanist Anthology*. London: Pemberton.

Lacan, J. (1964/1973) *The Four Fundamental Concepts of Psycho-Analysis: The Seminar of Jacques Lacan, Book XI* (translated by A. Sheridan). Harmondsworth: Penguin.

Lacan, J. (1975/1998) *On Feminine Sexuality, The Limits of Love and Knowledge, 1972–1973: Encore, The Seminar of Jacques Lacan, Book XX* (translated by B. Fink). New York: Norton.

Lacan, J. (1981/1993) *The Psychoses: The Seminar of Jacques Lacan, Book III: 1955–1956* (translated with notes by R. Grigg). London/New York: Routledge.

Lacan, J. (1991/2007) *The Other Side of Psychoanalysis: The Seminar of Jacques Lacan, Book XVII* (translated by R. Grigg). New York: Norton.

Laclau, E. (1990) *New Reflections on the Revolution of Our Time*. London: Verso.

Laclau, E. (2000a) 'Constructing universality', in J. Butler, E. Laclau and S. Žižek, *Contingency, Hegemony, Universality: Contemporary Dialogues on the Left*. London: Verso.

Laclau, E. (2000b) 'Structure, history and the political', in J. Butler, E. Laclau and S. Žižek, *Contingency, Hegemony, Universality: Contemporary Dialogues on the Left*. London: Verso.

Laclau, E. (2000c) 'Identity and hegemony: The role of universality in the constitution of political logics', in J. Butler, E. Laclau and S. Žižek, *Contingency, Hegemony, Universality: Contemporary Dialogues on the Left*. London: Verso.

Laclau, E. and Mouffe, C. (1985) *Hegemony and Socialist Strategy*. London: Verso.

Laing, R.D. (1964) *Sanity, Madness and the Family: Families of Schizophrenics*. London: Tavistock.

Laing, R.D. (1965) *The Divided Self: An Existential Study in Sanity and Madness*. Harmondsworth: Penguin.

Lasch, C. (1978) *The Culture of Narcissism*. New York: Norton.

Lax, W.D. (1992) 'Postmodern thinking in a clinical practice', in S. McNamee and K.J. Gergen (eds) *Therapy as Social Construction*. London: Sage.

Leader, D. (1996) *Why Do Women Write More Letters Than They Post?* London: Faber & Faber.

Leader, D. (1997) *Promises Lovers Make When It Gets Late*. London: Faber & Faber.

Lerman, H. (1992) 'The limits of phenomenology: A feminist critique of the humanistic personality theories', in L.S. Brown and M. Ballou (eds) *Personality and Psychopathology: Feminist Reappraisals*. New York: Guilford Press.

Lévi-Strauss, C. (1963) 'Do dual organizations exist?', in C. Lévi-Strauss, *Structural Anthropology*. New York: Basic Books.

Littlewood, R. and Lipsedge, M. (1989) *Aliens and Alienists: Ethnic Minorities and Psychiatry* (second edition). London: Unwin Hyman.

Lobovits, D. and Freeman, J. C. (1993) 'Toward collaboration and accountability: Alternatives to the dominant discourse for understanding professional sexual exploitation', *Dulwich Centre Newsletter*, 3/4, 33–44.

Long, C. and Zietkiewicz, E. (2001) 'Unsettling meanings of madness: Competing constructions of South African insanity', in D. Hook and G. Eagle (eds) *Psychopathology and Social Prejudice*. Cape Town: University of Cape Town Press.

Lowson, D. (1994) 'Understanding professional thought disorder: A guide for service users and a challenge for professionals', *Asylum: Magazine for Democratic Psychiatry*, 8(2), 29–30.

MacCannell, J.F. (1986) *Figuring Lacan: Criticism and the Cultural Unconscious*. Beckenham: Croom Helm.

MacDonnell, D. (1986) *Theories of Discourse: An Introduction*. Oxford: Blackwell.

Macey, D. (1988) *Lacan in Contexts*. London: Verso.

Madigan, S. (1992) 'The application of Michel Foucault's philosophy in the problem externalizing discourse of Michael White', *Journal of Family Therapy*, 14, 265–279.

Madigan, S. and Epston, D. (1995) 'From "psy-chiatric gaze" to communities of concern: From professional monologue to dialogue', in S. Friedman (ed.) *The Reflecting Team in Action: Collaborative Practice in Family Therapy*. New York: Guilford Press.

Mandel, E. (1978) *From Stalinism to Eurocommunism: The Bitter Fruits of 'Socialism in One Country'*. London: New Left Books.

Marsh, P., Rosser, E. and Harré, R. (1974) *The Rules of Disorder*. London: Routledge & Kegan Paul.

Marx, K. (1845/1975) 'Concerning Feuerbach', in *Marx: Early Writings*. Harmondsworth: Pelican.

Maslow, A. (1973) *The Farther Reaches of Human Nature*. Harmondsworth: Penguin.

McKenzie, W. and Monk, G. (1997) 'Learning and teaching narrative ideas', in G. Monk, J. Winslade, K. Crocket and D. Epston (eds) *Narrative Therapy in Practice: The Archaeology of Hope*. San Francisco: Jossey-Bass Publishers.

McLeod, J. (1997) *Narrative and Psychotherapy*. London: Sage.

McNamee, S. and Gergen, K.J. (eds) (1992) *Therapy as Social Construction*. London: Sage.

Mead, G. H. (1934) *Mind, Self and Society: From the Standpoint of a Social Behaviorist*. Chicago: Chicago University Press.

Mercer, K. (1986) 'Racism and transcultural psychiatry', in P. Miller and N. Rose (eds) *The Power of Psychiatry*. Cambridge: Polity Press.

Middleton, D. and Edwards, D. (eds) (1990) *Collective Remembering*. London: Sage.

Minson, J. (1980) 'Strategies for socialists? Foucault's conception of power', *Economy and Society*, 9(1), 1–43.

Minuchin, S. (1974) *Families and Family Therapy*. London: Tavistock Press.

Mitchell, J. (1974) *Psychoanalysis and Feminism*. Harmondsworth: Pelican.

Monk, G., Winslade, J., Crocket, K. and Epston, D. (eds) (1997) *Narrative Therapy in Practice: The Archaeology of Hope*. San Francisco: Jossey-Bass Publishers.

Moscovici, S. (1976/2008) *Psychoanalysis: Its Image and Its Public*. Cambridge: Polity Press.

Mowbray, R. (1995) *The Case Against Psychotherapy Registration: A Conversation Issue for the Human Potential Movement.* London: Transmarginal Press.

Nevill, D.D. (ed.) (1977) *Humanistic Psychology: New Frontiers.* New York: Gardner Press Inc.

Newman, F. and Holzman, L. (1997) *The End of Knowing: A New Developmental Way of Learning.* London: Routledge.

Nobus, D. (2000) *Jacques Lacan and the Freudian Practice of Psychoanalysis.* London: Routledge.

Norris, C. (1990) *Deconstruction Theory and Practice.* London and New York: Routledge.

Norris, C. (1996) 'Deconstruction, post-modernism and the visual arts', in C. Norris and A. Benjamin (eds) *What Is Deconstruction?* London: Academy Editions.

Novack, G. (1983) *Humanism and Socialism.* New York: Pathfinder Press

Parker, I. (1989) *The Crisis in Modern Social Psychology, and How to End It.* London: Routledge

Parker, I. (1992) *Discourse Dynamics: Critical Analysis for Social and Individual Psychology.* London and New York: Routledge.

Parker, I. (1994) 'Reflexive research and the grounding of analysis: social psychology and the psy-complex', *Journal of Community and Applied Social Psychology,* 4, 239–252.

Parker, I. (1995) 'Michel Foucault, psychologist', *The Psychologist,* 8(11), 503–505.

Parker, I. (1997a) 'Discursive psychology', in D. Fox and I. Prilleltensky (eds) *Critical Psychology: An Introduction.* London: Sage.

Parker, I. (1997b) *Psychoanalytic Culture: Psychoanalytic Discourse in Western Society.* London: Sage.

Parker, I. (1998a) 'Constructing and deconstructing psychotherapeutic discourse', *European Journal of Psychotherapy, Counselling and Health,* 1(1), 77–90.

Parker, I. (ed.) (1998b) *Social Constructionism, Discourse and Realism.* London: Sage.

Parker, I. (1999a) 'Critical psychology: Critical links', *Annual Review of Critical Psychology,* 1, 3–18.

Parker, I. (ed.) (1999b) *Deconstructing Psychotherapy.* London: Sage.

Parker, I. (1999c) 'Psychology and Marxism: Dialectical opposites?', in W. Maiers, B. Bayer, B. Duarte Esgalhado, R. Jorna and E. Schraube (eds) *Challenges to Theoretical Psychology.* Toronto: Captus University Publications.

Parker, I. (2005) *Qualitative Psychology: Introducing Radical Research.* Buckingham: Open University Press.

Parker, I. (2007) *Revolution in Psychology: Alienation to Emancipation.* London: Pluto Press.

Parker, I. (2008a) *Japan in Analysis: Cultures of the Unconscious.* London: Palgrave.

Parker, I. (2008b) 'Margins of resistance: Emotional illiteracy', *Qualitative Research in Psychology,* 5, 19–32.

Parker, I. (ed.) (2011a) *Critical Psychology: Critical Concepts in Psychology* (4 vols). Abingdon/New York: Routledge.

Parker, I. (2011b) *Lacanian Psychoanalysis: Revolutions in Subjectivity*. Abingdon/ New York: Routledge.

Parker, I. and the Bolton Discourse Network (1999) *Critical Textwork: An Introduction to Varieties of Discourse and Analysis*. Buckingham: Open University Press.

Parker, I. and Shotter, J. (eds) (1990) *Deconstructing Social Psychology*. London/ New York: Routledge.

Parker, I. Georgaca, E., Harper, D., McLaughlin, T. and Stowell-Smith, M. (1995) *Deconstructing Psychopathology*. London: Sage.

Phoenix, A (1994) 'Practising feminist research: The intersection of gender and "race" in the research process', in M. Maynard and J. Purvis (eds) *Researching Women's Lives from a Feminist Perspective*. London: Taylor & Francis.

Pilgrim, D. (1992) 'Psychotherapy and political evasions', in W. Dryden and C. Feltham (eds) *Psychotherapy and Its Discontents*. Buckingham: Open University Press.

Pilgrim, D. (1997) *Psychotherapy and Society*. London: Sage.

Pilkington, S. and Fraser, N. (1992) 'Exposing secret biographies', *Dulwich Centre Newsletter*, 1, 12–17.

Popper, K. (1959) *The Logic of Scientific Discovery*. London: Hutchinson.

Popper, K. (1963) *Conjectures and Refutations: The Growth of Scientific Knowledge*. London: Routledge & Kegan Paul.

Potter, J. (1998) 'Fragments in the realization of relativism', in I. Parker (ed.) *Social Constructionism, Discourse and Realism*. London: Sage.

Potter, J. and Wetherell, M. (1987) *Discourse and Social Psychology: Beyond Attitudes and Behaviour*. London: Sage.

Prilleltensky, I. and Fox, D. (1997) 'Introducing critical psychology: Values, assumptions, and the status quo', in D. Fox and I. Prilleltensky (eds) *Critical Psychology: An Introduction*. London: Sage.

Racevskis, K. (1983) *Michel Foucault and the Subversion of Intellect*. Ithaca, NY: Cornell University Press.

Ramon, S. and Giannichedda, M. (eds) (1989) *Psychiatry in Transition: The British and Italian Experiences*. London: Pluto Press.

Reason, P. and Rowan, J. (eds) (1981) *Human Inquiry: A Sourcebook for New Paradigm Research*. Chichester: Wiley.

Reicher, S.D. (1982) 'The determination of collective behaviour', in H. Tajfel (ed.) *Social Identity and Intergroup Relations*. Cambridge: Cambridge University Press.

Reicher, S. and Parker, I. (1993) 'Psychology politics resistance: The birth of a new organization', *Journal of Community and Applied Social Psychology*, 3, 77–80.

Richardson, F.C. and Fowers, B.J. (1997) 'Critical theory, postmodernism, and hermeneutics: Insights for critical psychology', in D. Fox and I. Prilleltensky (eds) *Critical Psychology: An Introduction*. London: Sage.

Riikonen, E. and Smith, G. (1997) *Re-Imagining Therapy: Living Conversations and Relational Knowing*. London: Sage.

Roberts, J. (2001) 'Review of *Contingency, Hegemony, Unversality*', *Radical Philosophy*, 105, 48–51.

Robertson, R. (1995) 'Glocalization: Time-space and homogeneity-heterogeneity', in M. Featherstone, S. Lash and R. Robertson (eds) *Global Modernities*. London: Sage.

Rogers, C. (1961) *On Becoming a Person: A Therapist's View of Psychotherapy*. London: Constable.

Romme, M. and Escher, A. (1993) *Accepting Voices*. London: MIND.

Rose, N. (1985) *The Psychological Complex: Psychology, Politics and Society in England 1869–1939*. London: Routledge & Kegan Paul.

Rose, N. (1990) 'Psychology as a "social" science', in I. Parker and J. Shotter (eds) *Deconstructing Social Psychology*. London: Routledge.

Rose, N. (1991) *Governing the Soul: The Shaping of the Private Self*. London/New York: Routledge.

Rosenthal, R. (1966) *Experimenter Effects in Behavioral Research*. New York: Appleton-Century-Crofts.

Roth, S. and Epston, D. (1996) 'Consulting the problem about the problematic relationship: an exercise for experiencing a relationship with an externalized problem', in M.F. Hoyt (ed.) *Constructive Therapies II*. New York: Guilford.

Rowan, J. (1994) *A Guide to Humanistic Psychology* (second edition). London: Association for Humanistic Psychology in Britain.

Rowbotham, S., Segal, L. and Wainwright, H. (1979/2013) *Beyond the Fragments: Feminism and the Making of Socialism*. Pontypool: Merlin Press.

Ryan, M. (1982) *Marxism and Deconstruction: A Critical Articulation*. Baltimore: Johns Hopkins University Press.

Said, E. (1983) *The World, the Text and the Critic*. Cambridge, MA: Harvard University Press.

Sarup, M. (1993) *Post-structuralism and Postmodernism*. Athens, GA: The University of Georgia Press.

Saussure, F. de (1915/1974) *Course in General Linguistics*. Glasgow: Fontana/Collins.

Sawacki, J. (1991) *Disciplining Foucault: Feminism, Power and the Body*. London: Routledge.

Selvini, M., Boscolo, L., Cecchin, G. and Prata, G. (1978) *Paradox and Counterparadox*. New York: Aronson.

Seu, I.B. and Heenan, M.C. (eds) (1998) *Feminism and Psychotherapy: Reflections on Contemporary Theories and Practices*. London: Sage.

Shotter, J. (1975) *Images of Man in Psychological Research*. London: Methuen.

Shotter, J. (1980) 'Action, joint action and intentionality', in M. Brenner (ed.) *The Structure of Action*. Oxford: Basil Blackwell.

Shotter, J. (1983) 'Hermeneutic Interpretative Theory', in R. Harré and R. Lamb (eds) *Encyclopaedic Dictionary of Psychology*. Oxford: Basil Blackwell.

Shotter, J. (1984) *Social Accountability and Selfhood*. Oxford: Basil Blackwell.

Shotter, J. (1993) *Cultural Politics of Everyday Life*. Buckingham: Open University Press.

Siegfried, J. (ed.) (1995) *Therapeutic and Everyday Discourse as Behavior Change: Towards a MicroAnalysis in Psychotherapy Process Research*. New York: Ablex.

Simblett, G.J. (1997) 'Narrative approaches to psychiatry', in G. Monk, J. Winslade, K. Crocket and D. Epston (eds) *Narrative Therapy in Practice: The Archaeology of Hope*. San Francisco, CA: Jossey-Bass.

Smith, A.M. (1998) *Laclau and Mouffe: The Radical Democratic Imaginary*. London: Routledge.

Soyland, A.J. and Kendall, G. (1997) 'Abusing Foucault: Methodology, critique and subversion', *British Psychological Society History and Philosophy of Psychology Section Newsletter*, 25, 9–17.

Spivak, G.C. (1988) 'Can the subaltern speak?', in C. Nelson and L. Grossberg (eds) *Marxism and the Interpretation of Culture*. Urbana: University of Illinois Press.

Spivak, G.C. (1990) 'Practical politics of the open end', in S. Harasym (ed.) *The Postcolonial Critic: Interviews, Strategies, Dialogues*. London: Routledge.

Stacey, K. (1997) 'Alternative metaphors for externalizing conversations', *Gecko*, 1, 29–51.

Stanley, L. and Wise, S. (1983) *Breaking Out: Feminist Consciousness and Feminist Research*. London: Routledge & Kegan Paul.

Stavrakakis, Y. (1999) *Lacan and the Political*. London: Routledge.

Swartz, S. (1996) 'Shrinking: A postmodern perspective on psychiatric case histories', *South African Journal of Psychology,* 26(3), 150–156.

Tamasese, K. and Waldegrave, C. (1996) 'Culture and gender accountability in the "Just Therapy" approach', in C. McLean, M. Carey and C. White (eds) *Men's Ways of Being*. Boulder, CO: Westview Press.

Ussher, J. (1991) *Women's Madness: Misogyny or Mental Illness?* Hemel Hempstead: Harvester Wheatsheaf.

Waldegrave, C. (1990) 'Just therapy', *Dulwich Centre Newsletter*, 1, 6–46.

Wann, T.W. (ed.) (1964) *Behaviorism and Phenomenology: Contrasting Bases for Modern Psychology*. Chicago: Chicago University Press

Waterhouse, R. (1993) '"Wild women don't have the blues": A feminist critique of "personcentred" counselling and therapy', *Feminism and Psychology*, 3(1), 55–71.

Weedon, C. (1987) *Feminist Practice and Post-structuralist Theory*. Oxford: Blackwell.

White, M. (1989a) 'The externalizing of the problem and the re-authoring of the lives and relationships', in M. White, *Selected Papers*. Adelaide: Dulwich Centre Publications.

White, M. (1989b) 'The process of questioning: a therapy of literary merit?', in M. White, *Selected Papers*. Adelaide: Dulwich Centre Publications.

White, M. (1991) 'Deconstruction and therapy', *Dulwich Centre Newsletter*, 3, 21–40.

White, M. (1995a) *Re-Authoring Lives: Interviews and Essays*. Adelaide: Dulwich Centre Publications.

White, M. (1995b) 'A conversation about accountability', in M. White, *Re-Authoring Lives: Interviews and Essays*. Adelaide: Dulwich Centre Publications.

White, M. (1995c) 'Reflecting teamwork as definitional ceremony', in M. White, *Re-Authoring Lives: Interviews and Essays*. Adelaide: Dulwich Centre Publications.

White, M. and Epston, D. (1990) *Narrative Means to Therapeutic Ends*. Adelaide: Dulwich Centre Publications.

Winslade, J., Crocket, K. and Monk, G. (1997) 'The therapeutic relationship', in G. Monk, J. Winslade, K. Crocket and D. Epston (eds) *Narrative Therapy in Practice: The Archaeology of Hope*. San Francisco: Jossey-Bass Publishers.

Wood, D.C. (1979) 'An introduction to Derrida', *Radical Philosophy*, 21, 18–28.

Woolfe, R. (1985) 'What is counselling? Counselling and counselling psychology as an ideology', *BPS Counselling Section Newsletter*, 3(2), 4–16.

Woolgar, S. (1988) *Science: The Very Idea*. Chichester: Ellis Horwood.

Young, R.M. (1994) *Mental Space*. London: Process Press.

Yuval-Davis, N. (2006) 'Intersectionality and feminist politics', *European Journal of Women's Studies*, 13(3), 193–209.

Zaretsky, E. (1976) *Capitalism, the Family and Personal Life*. London: Pluto Press.

Žižek, S. (1990) 'Beyond discourse-analysis', in E. Laclau, *New Reflections on the Revolution of Our Time*. London: Verso.

Žižek, S. (1999) *The Ticklish Subject: The Absent Centre of Political Ontology*. London: Verso.

Žižek, S. (2000a) 'Holding the place', in J. Butler, E. Laclau and S. Žižek, *Contingency, Hegemony, Universality: Contemporary Dialogues on the Left*. London: Verso.

Žižek, S. (2000b) '*Da Capo senza Fine*', in J. Butler, E. Laclau and S. Žižek, *Contingency, Hegemony, Universality: Contemporary Dialogues on the Left*. London: Verso.

Žižek, S. (2000c) 'Class struggle or postmodernism? Yes, please!', in J. Butler, E. Laclau and S. Žižek, *Contingency, Hegemony, Universality: Contemporary Dialogues on the Left*. London: Verso.

Index